MY JOURNEY TO JOY

OTHER PRODUCTS

To order Cindy Johnson's CDs visit:
www.cindyjohnson4hisgloryministries.com

My Journey
to
Joy

Cindy Johnson

Endorsement by Gina Johnson

My Journey to Joy is so needed by people who have had their faith shaken by the tough circumstances of life. This very personal insight into Cindy's pain and disappointments is a wonderful example of how God comforts us in our trials "that we may be able to comfort them which are in trouble by the comfort wherewith we ourselves are comforted of God." Cindy's faith takes her through her storms instead of around them. is amazing book gets "two ARMS up" in praise to Jesus for being our very present help in time of trouble.

My Journey to Joy

Copyright © 2014 by Cindy Johnson

ISBN: 978-1-934447-76-5

Published by Whispering Pines Publishing, Shoals, Indiana

All scripture references are from the King James Version unless stated otherwise.

Printed in the United States of America by Country Pines Printing in Shoals, Indiana

Dedication

**This book is dedicated in loving memory of
Jacob Anthony Johnson**
5-2-2004 – 5-4-2004

Forever in My Heart

Inspired by Jacob's great-grandfather, Rev. Bert F. Ford
Written by Cindy Johnson

A soul intended for Heaven's best
That never knew life's trials and tests
Never knew the tears of sorrow
Nor had to fight the wars of tomorrow

So I'll let you go
While Heaven holds you for a while
I'll hold on to hope until I see your smile
And though right now we have to be apart
I'll hold you forever in my heart.

You've reached the place that I long to be
Singing with the angels on bended knee
One day soon I'll join you in the song
And sing with you around God's throne

Dedication Continued ...

To Isaac, Mommy's little man. From the moment I saw you, I loved you. From the moment I held you, I knew I was holding a miracle straight from Heaven. Your life is a constant reminder to me that God still works miracles! You were the "missing piece of the puzzle" in my life; a perfect fit; a perfect design from God himself. Out of all the baby boys in the whole wide world, God chose you for me. And, out of all the moms in the whole wide world, God chose me for you. From the beginning of time, God knew that you would be mine. You came along according to God's timing and helped fill the empty places in my heart with your love. *(2 Samuel 22:31, As for God, his way is perfect.)*
~ Unexpected, but selected! ~

To Anthony, my husband. For 25 years I've had the privilege of having you by my side. You are a true "hero" of the faith and my very best friend. Your faith has remained constant and has never wavered. You have been a rock to lean on and a steady stream of security in my weakest moments. Thank you for cheering me on to brighter days and for loving me unconditionally. I am so thankful that God brought us together. We have something special that the world can't take away! A good man is a rare find, and you are that to me.

To my Lord and Savior, Jesus Christ. I am blessed beyond measure with your love and the peace that you alone can give. You are the only one that can heal, save, deliver, and redeem. I am most grateful for the gift of salvation. May I never lose sight of Calvary's scene and the wonder of the cross. May it remain alive in me so that I will live my life more consecrated to you, take up my meager cross, and follow wherever you may lead me along my journey of faith. I have found true joy and contentment in serving you!

Table of Contents

Acknowledgments

Words could never adequately express my thanks:

✦ To the many friends and supporters who stood by me, expressed their care in countless ways, and prayed me through the tough times.

✦ To my awesome family who cried with me, laughed with me, and prayed me through to brighter days.

✦ To my wonderful husband and son who have supported me during the process of completing this book. I promise I will clean the house and play football with you again after this is all finished!

✦ To my sister-n-love (Lisa) and my friend (Elaine) who both spent many hours helping me edit this book.

✦ To my new friends at Country Pines Printing for all of your help in creating such a beautiful finished product.

✦ To Pastor Randy Johnson and Assoc. Pastor Mark Potter for your anointed Sunday sermons which have inspired me to write some of the chapters in my book.

✦ To my friend, Adina Benton Bowman, who has encouraged me to share my story for His glory.

- ✦ To my mom for always believing in me and rejoicing with me in my many victories along the way.

- ✦ To my Heavenly Father whose love never fails. It is my deepest desire that your excellent greatness will be illuminated to all who read this story.

Introduction

Whether you are dealing with infertility, the death of a loved one, feelings of depression and anxiety, or just need a faith boost, the Lord has led you to this book. You will find words of encouragement and hope for your broken heart.

My personal journals and my song lyrics which were inspired by the Holy Spirit are included in each chapter. You can look into the windows of my heart as I dealt with sixteen years of infertility and the grief for the child I could not have. We will travel down a road towards triumph as I share how God miraculously sent us our baby boy. Then we will explore an uncharted path of tragedy, when our miracle baby passed away shortly after his birth.

We will walk hand in hand, down my path of depression to my destiny of victory! Experience with me the unexpected while struggling with anxiety and the deliverance that God gave me from my fears!

As the story unfolds, you will see firsthand how God proved Himself faithful to what He had promised me.

This I recall to my mind, therefore have I hope. It is of the Lord's mercies that we are not consumed, because his compassions fail not. They are new every morning: great is thy faithfulness. But

11

though he causes grief, yet will he have compassion according to the multitude of his mercies. For he doth not afflict willingly nor grieve the children of men.

Additionally, you will be reminded of God's sustaining grace and protection and see how He brought my family through yet another crisis when a fire totally destroyed our home.

By the time you finish walking this journey with me, I believe that you will understand how God can turn your tragedy into triumph, turn your pain into praise, give you a happy ending to your personal journey, and enable you to share your story for His glory!

I pray that the Lord will fill your heart and mind with hope as you read what I have been inspired by the Holy Spirit to share from His heart, for His sake … for His glory!

Lord, may my life be an open book for the world to see your faithfulness, your power, your glory, and the joy that you alone can give to all those who choose to believe!

Allow your faith to stretch beyond the unseen and let's get started on our journey to joy!

Chapter 1

My Journey to Joy Begins

"A merry heart doeth good like a medicine: but a broken spirit drieth the bones" Proverbs 17:22.

As far back as I can remember my dream had always been to become a mother and have a family of my own. That was simple enough, so I thought. Surely God would allow those dreams to be fulfilled. After all, I was a Christian and married to a wonderful, godly man of faith. We were married in November 1988 and planned to raise a house full of children. We even chose the names of our children when we dated. However, we never imagined that God would take us down such a long and winding road laced with disappointment and grief. As we would learn many years later, He had a better plan in mind.

Approximately six years into our marriage, we felt it was time to begin fertility testing. Our doctors could not find any physiological problems with either of us. This was good news. However, this seemed to frustrate me even more. How could I fix something that didn't need fixing? I struggled on a daily basis, eventually allowing this situation to consume every thought.

I could not understand why the Lord would deprive my husband and me of such a privilege. After all, if children are a blessing from the Lord then why wouldn't He bless us? What had we done wrong? Did God know what I was feeling? Surely if He did, He would answer my cry of desperation in *my* time and not allow me to endure the "waiting room" of uncertainty.

My tears of agony began to drain me physically, spiritually, and emotionally. I lacked true joy and contentment. After sixteen years of marriage, I was still grieving for the child I could not have. I felt unsettled, dissatisfied, and incomplete.

I eventually allowed myself to sink into depression. I was living in my own bubble and it was about to burst. My marriage was being affected, and I almost found myself becoming a "bitter party of one."

I became very good at faking a smile when my friends shared with me their wonderful news that they were expecting. My heart was actually sinking inside. Their news only reminded me that my arms were empty and that their dreams were being fulfilled. My mind was filled with the question, "What about me?"

Chapter 2

Bending to His Will

"Thou compassest my path and my lying down, and art acquainted with all my ways. For there is not a word in my tongue, but, lo, O Lord, thou knowest it altogether. Thou hast beset me behind and before, and laid thine hand upon me. Such knowledge is too wonderful for me, it is high, I cannot attain unto it" Psalms 139:3-6.

Life was all about me during this long period of infertility. I was obsessed with the fact that I wasn't getting what I wanted, and I was tired of pretending to be happy about it. My actions were similar to that of a child that doesn't get his or her way. The situation was out of my reach and out of my control. Unfortunately, it has taken me years to finally realize that God is ultimately in control of all things. He gets the last word and that really is a "good" thing because He does all things well and makes no mistakes.

Rather than asking the important question, "What does God want for me?" I was too busy asking the question, "What about me?" I never really considered that I wasn't trusting in the One who knew me best and never sought His perfect will in the matter of having children. It was my way or bust!

There is never a time while traveling this faith journey that God doesn't know every detail in our lives that concerns us. What concerns us, concerns Him as well. He gently leads us down unexpected paths to change our perspective and sometimes our attitude.

Just as our earthly parents correct us in love and want us to grow and mature as responsible adults, our Heavenly Father wishes to do the same for us spiritually. He does not glory in our pain, but uses our experiences to teach us His faithfulness. He loves us too much not to correct us when we are going down a path that could somehow bring harm to our eternal souls. We attempt to help God and rather than leaning on His understanding, we lean on our own.

I am sure that He has looked down at me many times wondering why I just couldn't trust Him to work things out in His time and in His way. How many times have we heard a parent correcting their child saying, "Trust me. I know what is best for you right now." God knows what is best for us as well. Sometimes He has to break our will in order for us learn to bend to His will and submit to His ways.

God is referred to as our Shepherd in Scripture. Shepherds have to lead their sheep, and are responsible for their safety. When a sheep goes astray, it is in danger of predators, starvation, and death. The shepherd's heart is grieved. He has no choice but to inflict pain in order for the sheep to learn to follow more closely to Him, thus saving his life. The sheep's leg must be broken. As the shepherd tends to the sheep with the broken leg, the sheep learns to lean on his master and begins to trust him in a ways as never before. The sheep becomes dependent on the shepherd. The innocent sheep slowly learns to bend his ear to his master's voice and begins to trust him. He realizes the need to stay close to him for guidance and protection and no longer ventures out away from the flock. He has learned thru the pain the importance of bending to his master's voice.

Isaiah 40:11 says, *"He shall feed his flock like a shepherd; he shall gather the lambs with his arm, and carry them in his bosom, and shall gently lead those that are with young."*

Lord, may we constantly be willing to bend to Your ways and not ours. May our hearts be yielded to Your plans for our lives. May we realize that you only want what is best for us as you gently lead us along in paths of righteousness for Your name's sake.

Psalm 23

The Lord is my shepherd; I shall not want.

He maketh me to lie down in green pastures: he leadeth me beside the still waters.

He restoreth my soul: he leadeth me in the paths of righteousness for his name's sake.

Yea, though I walk through the valley of the shadow of death, I will fear no evil: for thou art with me; thy rod and thy staff they comfort me.

Thou preparest a table before me in the presence of mine enemies: thou anointest my head with oil; my cup runneth over.

Surely goodness and mercy shall follow me all the days of my life: and I will dwell in the house of the Lord forever.

—King James Version

Chapter 3

It's Hard to Trust

"Now faith is the substance of things hoped for and the evidence of things not seen" Hebrews 11:1.

I was brought up in a Christian home and was encouraged to trust in the Lord with all my heart. Nevertheless, I had not yet learned how to put these biblical standards into practice. My faith was very shallow and innocently so. You see, I had never faced a storm; therefore, I hadn't learned how to "trust" God. I hadn't learned how to bend my ear to the Master's voice and His ways.

I was asking Him plenty of questions, but wasn't getting any answers; at least, not the answers that I wanted. This proved to be a constant struggle within me. I was tired of waiting for Him to answer my prayer. I remember my husband's grandfather saying many times that there are three answers to prayer; one is yes, one is no, and one is wait awhile.

No one likes to wait. Whether it's waiting in long lines in the grocery store or waiting for our deepest dreams and desires to be attained, we don't want to wait.

So, what do we do in the meantime? What do we do while we are in the "waiting room" of life and find ourselves in a place on our journey where we don't want to be? As Christians, we can look to God's Word for the answer, and that is to trust in the Lord.

Proverbs 3:5-6 encourages us to *"Trust in the Lord with all thine heart and lean not unto thine own understanding. In all thy ways, acknowledge Him and He shall direct thy paths."*

Oh, how difficult that is and why is that? Why do we doubt that our Heavenly father is working all things for our good when He is the one who created the universe? Sometimes we have a difficult time wrapping our minds around this Biblical truth. The Bible even tells us that His ways are so much higher than ours—more than our minds can comprehend.

This is where our faith begins to take root on our journey to joy. Yes, faith is the key. It takes faith in order for us to trust. However, our faith can become weak when we can't see the end result of our prayers. It is very important that we practice our faith in these situations.

Even when we think of all the promises that God has made in His Word and remember that He has never broken one of them, we still doubt Him at times. The following journal entry is proof of that:

Journal Entry May 2001

Well, the month of April has been a tough one. However, I feel like I am almost flying on mended wings again. It is a roller-coaster ride of emotions dealing with infertility. Being barren makes me feel incomplete and empty. I can't help but wonder if and when God will answer my prayer. Sometimes, it feels like He's not even

20

listening. I know His Word tells me that He hears my prayer. However, my faith is lacking. It is hard to trust in the unknown! Many times I am overwhelmed with feelings of hopelessness. There are no more tears left for me to cry.

Psalms 40 says, *"I waited patiently for the Lord; and he inclined to me, and has heard my cry. He has brought me up out of a horrible pit, out of the miry clay, and set my feet upon a rock, and established my steps. He has put a new song in my mouth. Praise to our God; many will see it and fear, and will trust in the Lord. Blessed is the man who makes the Lord His trust."*

While writing this book the Holy Spirit spoke words of comfort to me concerning prayer and faith. I would like to share this journal with you.

Journal Entry April 13, 2012

Trust me. I've provided all of your needs in the past, so why do you doubt me now? Remember, I am all sufficient and my mercies are new each morning. Don't doubt my power or my ability. Give to me your everything; your wants, your desires, and I'll give you more than you could ever ask or imagine! The Israelites doubted me when they were hungry, even after seeing many of my miracles. They turned to the left and to the right, worshiping false idols. I am the one true God and I do not, and cannot, and will not ever fail you. Trust me in all things, and I will provide exactly what you need.

The more time that we spend in prayer, the more our faith will increase, and the more we will find ourselves trusting in God's Word. It is in those intimate times with Him that He opens our hearts to supernaturally see the things that we couldn't see before. Prayer increases our faith. Faith helps us to trust Him more.

Lord, help us to "wait" patiently and trust in you even in times of uncertainty. May the light of your eternal love continue to guide us on our journey to joy.

Learning How to Lean

In April of 2003, my husband and I received a phone call from a friend of ours asking us if we would like to adopt a baby girl. The baby was in South Carolina and was a result of an affair. Of course, I thought this was the miracle that God had for us and was ready to get on the next plane flight to bring this baby home.

However, my husband decided it was not the right timing in our lives and was uneasy about the idea of adoption. Needless to say, I did not take this very well and did not understand. My heart was aching, and my arms were empty. My emotions were running high. I somehow managed to tell him I would trust that his decision was the right one and would try to accept it and go on. Well, that was easier said than done! I said that with my mouth, but not with my heart.

The next day I came home from work on my lunch break and had a long talk with the Lord. He reminded me of what He'd promised me in May of 2002. The following journal explains:

Journal Entry May 5, 2002

What a wonderful church service we had tonight! As the pastor was praying for me, the Spirit of the Lord whispered the words … "Get ready." A group of ladies also prayed for me, and one in particular who did not know me, or my situation, said very softly, "The Lord is going to give you the petition of your heart, and it will be in a way that you will least expect it." This was similar to what God had told Hannah when she was longing for a child. Thank you, God, for revealing this to me. Thank you for your faithfulness and hearing my prayers. Use me, Lord.

Journal Entry April 4, 2003 (almost one year later)

As I was praying today at home the Lord met with me in a very powerful way. I cried out from my heart once again and told God just how I felt, asking Him for guidance and the grace to accept the decision that Anthony had made about this baby girl. I picked up my journal and flipped through the pages when I remembered documenting some things that God had spoken to me. I wept and thanked Him for reminding me what He had said He was going to do in my life in that special church service. I then opened my Bible asking God for yet another sign; a sign of confirmation. My eyes fell upon the words from Isaiah 46:11 which said, *"Indeed I have spoken it; I will also bring it to pass; I have purposed it; I will also do it."* What an amazing confirmation for my prayer. Thank you, Lord, for your faithfulness. Thank you for your Word.

The pastor's message this week was about believing and claiming what God has spoken to you.

He Still Speaks ...

I am a firm believer that God speaks to His children. If we listen, He will speak things to our hearts through His Spirit and His Word. He often uses other people at times to confirm His Word.

May the Lord help us to be sensitive to His spirit and listen for His still small voice. God wants to talk to us, but we have to be willing to listen for as long as it takes to receive our answer.

As Christians, we can hold on to God's promises and believe that He will work things out in His time and His way, praying according to God's will and not ours. It is something that we have to put into practice on our faith journey.

Even though I felt God had made these promises to me, it was still hard at times to hold on to them. I would become weak in my faith even still. Sometimes, I felt like I was holding on by a thread.

As I have already mentioned, it's difficult to have faith before the answer comes because you don't know the when, if, or how your answer will come. It's like walking blindly in the dark not knowing how to take the next step when suddenly our gentle Shepherd takes our hand and says, "Walk with me, this is the way."

That's what God can do for us in our times of weakness when we can't see the whole picture. He holds our hands leading us along and encourages us to take one step at a time. Sometimes our steps are small, and sometimes we take two steps backward. However, we can lean on Him to lead us on our faith journey.

Many days I felt despondent and felt like giving up, but then God's sweet Holy Spirit would comfort me and remind me that He was with me. Eventually, I felt myself walking those baby steps of faith again.

It's a day by day choice. What will you believe? Will you choose to believe that God has your best interest at heart? Or, will you choose to walk away from His hand that is outstretched to pull you up again so that you can continue to travel this journey walking by faith?

When doubts arise, and they will, remember that God knows your circumstances and is fully aware of every detail that concerns you and every burden that weighs you down.

Scripture tells us to lay aside every weight that so easily besets us. So lay your burdens down at His feet. He is your burden bearer. Give Him your tears, your disappointments and your broken dreams.

Remember, God is for you—not against you! Trust in His Word and choose to believe every promise that it holds.

Keep Believing

(copyright 2013)

You wonder if the Lord has heard your prayer.
Is He listening? Does He really care?
But when you pray and reach the throne room,
You will hear His still small voice,
And without a doubt you'll know that He is there.
He was always there.

Refrain

So keep believing.
Your answer's on the way.
Keep holding on to what the Lord has promised you.
For God is faithful,

And He'll do just what He said He'd do.
Keep believing,
Keep believing.

Your healing has begun.
Reach out and claim it.
He who began the work in you
Is more than able to complete it.
Stand on His promises
'Til your battle has been won,
And you will stand amazed at all that He has done,
All the Lord has done.

Chapter 4

Good News!

Several months had passed, and we found ourselves in the month of October 2003. My doctor recommended a laparoscopy and a D and C that month. Everything went fine, and after the surgery, the doctor told my husband that he didn't see any reason why I shouldn't be able to conceive.

We decided to proceed with foreign adoption from China and sent for the application to start the process in November. Just a few short weeks later, we received some very exciting news; news that we had been waiting to hear for 16 years! My nurse called me with the results of my pregnancy test and it was positive. I was finally pregnant! She had to put the doctor on the phone to fully convince me.

The following journal writing describes my feelings that day:

December 17, 2003

Today marks a very special day in our lives. I have just found out I am pregnant. All the years of waiting are finally over. I never dreamed this day would unfold like it has. When my doctor told me the results were positive all I could do was cry tears of joy!

Everyone is telling us that this is our Christmas miracle. The blood work revealed that I may even have twins. Thank you God for your faithfulness to me and for fulfilling your promise! I can hardly believe this! It is amazing how things can change so quickly.

Dear God, please help everything to go smoothly in this pregnancy. Touch this child/children in my womb and make him/her healthy and strong. May they grow up serving you and testifying of your love. Help us to be Godly parents giving us wisdom and guidance. Thank you, God, for this miracle! We can finally use the names we chose 16 years ago for our child. Will it be Jacob or Sarah or both?

A sonogram would later reveal that we were having a boy, and his due date was July 31, 2004. Our Jacob would soon be in our arms, and life would be sweeter! The years of longing for a child were over. No more empty arms!

The months passed, and I felt wonderful. I did everything I was supposed to do to take care of myself and my precious little baby. As you can imagine, we were making big plans for Jacob and could not wait to see his little face and hear his cry. His kicks came in the wee hours of the morning, and he was becoming quite active.

Like some pregnant women, I was feisty and quite temperamental. Actually, that was not my personality, and I really didn't like myself. So, during a Sunday night altar service, I went up for prayer asking God to change my attitude. As the pastor began to pray, the Spirit of the Lord whispered these words to me. "Do not fear. Do not be afraid, for the things that will take place are to bring glory and honor to my name."

I remember thinking to myself over the next few days, "I wonder if the Lord is trying to prepare me for something?" I would find out just a few weeks later what that something was.

The Unexpected Storm

The day was April 21, 2004, and I went into labor. I was transported by ambulance to Arnold Palmer Hospital in Orlando, Florida, never realizing what I would be facing. The ride to the hospital was long and bumpy. It would prove to be the beginning of the unexpected storm on my faith journey. I was scared to death. This was not supposed to be happening. After all, this was our miracle baby. We had been waiting for 16 years, longing for him to come into our lives.

I remember talking with the EMT as she sat beside me. She tried to assure me that everything would be fine, but her words did not bring me the comfort that I needed. It would take a supernatural touch from the Lord. I needed Him to come to my rescue. I needed to hear the Shepherd's voice comforting me in my storm. As the tears rolled down my cheeks I cried out to the Lord for His help. His peace swept over me as He reminded me of His faithfulness though the words of this old hymn of the church written by Thomas Chisolm:

Great Is Thy Faithfulness

Great is Thy faithfulness, O God my Father,
There is no shadow of turning with Thee;
Thou changest not, Thy compassions, they fail not
As Thou hast been Thou forever wilt be.

Refrain

Great is Thy faithfulness! Great is Thy faithfulness!
Morning by morning new mercies I see;
All I have needed Thy hand hath provided.
Great is Thy faithfulness, Lord, unto me!

I sang it in the ambulance. The EMT grew quiet. I believe she knew that I needed a higher source of help. Finally, I arrived at the hospital. The doctors gave me encouraging news. They felt like everything would be alright and told me to be patient and to get used to my room because I would be there until the end of the pregnancy. I told them that I did not care what I had to do as long as Jacob was going to be okay.

They monitored his every move and his heartbeat. All the nurses and doctors told me what a strong heartbeat he had and what a "fighter" he was. "He's strong," they would say.

I had a lot of time on my hands, so I decided to journal my thoughts each day. The following is my journal writing a few days after I was admitted into the hospital:

Journal writing 4/27/04

Today is April 27th, which makes 26 weeks and 4 days into my pregnancy. Thank the Lord for each additional day that Jacob stays put. Each day is one more

31

that he can grow a little stronger, and his lungs can develop. Everyone is praying for us, and I am thankful for all the support we have. Thank God for His faithfulness that He continues to show to me even now! His mercies are new every morning—all I have needed thy hand has provided. Great is thy faithfulness, Lord, unto me.

I know that God is making me stronger through this and is teaching me to trust Him in all things. *"The Lord is not slack concerning his promise, as some men count slackness, but is longsuffering to usward"* II Peter 3:9. *"O Lord, thou are my God; I will exalt thee, I will praise thy name, for thou has done wonderful things, thy counsels of old are faithfulness and truth."* Isaiah 25:1.

Yes, God is faithful and we can depend on His promises. I just didn't realize how much I would have to rely on His Word as the days went by. I really thought that Jacob would be fine and that this was how God would receive the glory.

The following journal writing is about a week after I was admitted into the hospital.

Journal writing 4/29/04

Thank the Lord for another day! Jacob's heartbeat continues to remain strong. They are still monitoring him around the clock. His heart rate sometimes falls into the 60's. My frame of mind is still positive, and I know it is a result of all the prayer that is taking place for us even right now! I am holding on to God's promise to me. I just know that Jacob is a special miracle from the Lord and that He will use Jacob's life to bring glory and honor to Him.

On May 2nd in the wee hours of the morning I woke up feeling feverish. Before long the doctors and nurses came in and said they were going to have to perform an emergency C-section. Jacob's heart rate was decreasing, and he was not active. Things didn't look good, but my hopes were still high.

Jacob Anthony Johnson was born on May 2nd weighing 2 pounds 8 ounces, and was 15 inches long. The nurses rolled him over to me after they cleaned him up. He was beautiful and perfect. What a blessed day; the day we had waited so long for!

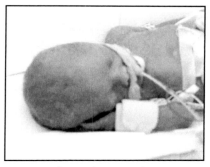

Jacob Anthony Johnson

My husband and I slept off and on through the night only to awaken to the beginning of a nightmare. Jacob's condition had worsened through the night, and he was given two blood transfusions. There was infection in his blood stream, and his lungs had not fully developed. The doctor informed my husband that Jacob would not live much longer, and we would need to make the decision to take him off of life support.

I remember sitting there with my husband in the neonatal unit looking at his frail little body and praying for a miracle. His vital signs would rise as I held him to my chest. We continued to pray as we waited for God to bring a healing to our precious little baby. We sang every hymn we could think of as we cradled him in our arms: "Won't It Be Wonderful There," "Jesus Loves Me," "How Beautiful Heaven Must Be" to name a few.

We talked to him as we cradled his frail little body, telling him how beautiful Heaven was going to be. If God didn't allow him to stay here with us, then he was going to beat us to the place that we had heard about all of our lives. He would beat us to the finish line.

I will never forget the pain that was written on the faces of our family as they stood with us beside Jacob. Their hearts ached for us. They, too, were praying for a miracle from Heaven.

The doctors told us that Jacob would only live for approximately 30 minutes after they took him off life support. However, he lived 8 precious hours, and I thank God for the time that He allowed my husband and me to hold him. 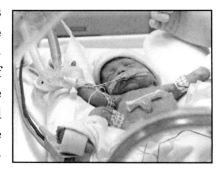 As I placed him against my chest to cradle him, his vital signs would improve drastically. The nurses would rush over to examine him, and after a little while his vital signs would regress. We held on until the very end hoping for God to perform a miracle!

God did perform a miracle, but just not the way we wanted. Jacob was ushered into Heaven by the angels on May 4, 2004. I held his precious little body until he took his last breath. We said our good byes, and I kissed my baby for the last time on this side of Heaven.

As my family took me back to my room, I remember the feeling of hopelessness that swept over my heart. I felt like God had forsaken me, and I wanted to die. My arms were empty and my baby was gone.

The grief was indescribable. I am certain that the entire floor of the hospital heard my desperate cries of agony. I cried, "Is this what I have waited all these years for? I want my baby!" It took the entire family to hold me up and calm me down enough to get me into the bed. This would prove to be the biggest test of my faith that I had ever faced.

As my husband wheeled me out of the hospital the next day, my arms were aching worse than the pain from my incision. I convinced the doctor to let me leave a day early. I couldn't bear hearing the newborn babies crying down the hall. This was not part of the plan. We were supposed to have our bundle of joy with us. There were no smiles. It was a solemn occasion.

The questions flooded my mind. How was I going to face the hurdles in front of me? How was I going to make it through this storm … this nightmare? As you can probably imagine the following days, weeks and months would be the hardest times that my family and I would ever have to face.

However, I am so thankful that God gave me a wonderful Christian husband whose faith did not waver through all of our pain. He was familiar with the loss of someone he loved and had experienced grief as a young child when his father was shot and killed in front of him at the age of 11 in a hunting accident. Instead of blaming God, he trusted God through his pain then, and now through the death of our son. I have never met a stronger man of faith than my husband. My faith, however, was not that strong.

All I knew was that my arms were empty, and I was hurting, and no one could "fix" it for me. No one except God, and that would take some time … as I allowed Him to.

You may be in the midst of an unexpected storm. Remember to look unto the hills where your help comes from. Your help comes from the Lord.

The following prayer has been one I have prayed in times that I didn't understand God's plan.

Lord, how do I pick up the pieces? There are thousands of shattered fragments. So many, that I don't think that anyone could ever put them back together. My heart feels ruined beyond recognition. Will I ever learn to live again when I'm barely hanging on to the promises I've learned in your Word? It will only be by your grace. Oh, I remember the word grace. Yes, Your grace is sufficient. How will I survive this part of my faith journey? Yes, I remember that word "faith." I've heard about it all my life. Help me find my faith, Lord. I am drowning in a river of tears. Remind me of your love for me. I cannot seem to find my way. Please point my heart towards the reality of Heaven. I can't take another step. I stand in need of your peace, a touch from you, a breath from Heaven that will soothe and reach the places deep within my heart that only you can reach.

We will all face storms at some point and there will be times when we feel like giving up. We just have to remember that God is in the midst of each storm and is standing with open arms to embrace us in our pain. I encourage you to run to Him and let Him be your refuge. We can all take comfort in the fact that when we are faithless in the midst of the storm, He is still faithful!

Chapter 6

Facing the Storm

I'd rather walk with Him in the dark, than walk alone in the light (Unknown).

It was May 6, the day before Jacob's funeral, and I was dreading what I had to face. This storm had not been on the radar of my life journey. I felt hopeless and felt as if I was drowning in a sea of misery.

My mother came across a passage of Scripture that morning and read it to me. It was Psalm 18. The words seemed to leap off the page and described how I was feeling. Later that afternoon my sister-in-law brought my attention to II Samuel 22. To my amazement, I found that it was the mirrored Scripture of Psalm 18. I realized that the Lord was bringing these Scriptures to help me in the days ahead. He was reminding me that He would not let me drown and that He would be my lifeline and strength in my time of trouble.

I read these passages all the way to the funeral the next day and held on to God's Word more than ever before. I knew everyone was praying for me, and I would learn firsthand what God's grace could do that day and in the days that would follow.

Psalms 18:1-6, 16-19, 28-29, 31-36, 46

(A song of victory that King David cried out to God in great distress—David realized that His help and deliverance came only from God.)

I love you, Lord, You are my strength. The Lord is my rock, my protection, my Savior. My God is my rock. I can run to him for safety. He is my shield and my saving strength, my defender. I will call to the Lord, who is worthy of praise, and I will be saved from my enemies. The rope of death came around me; the deadly rivers overwhelmed me. The ropes of death wrapped around me. The traps of death were before me. In my trouble I called to the Lord for help. From His temple He heard my voice. ***My call for help reached his ears.***

The Lord reached down from above and took me; he pulled me from the deep water. He saved me. The Lord protected me. He took me to a safe place. Because He delights in me, he saved me. *Lord you give light to my lamp. My God brightens the darkness around me. With your help I can advance through a troop. With your help I can jump over a wall. Who is God? Only the Lord. Who is the Rock? Only our God. God is my protection.* ***He makes me like a deer that does not stumble; He helps me stand on the steep mountains.*** *He trains my hands for battle so my arms can bend a bronze bow. You protect me with* *your saving shield. You support me with your right hand. You have stooped to make me great. You give me a better way to live, so I live as you want me to. The Lord lives! May my rock be praised. Praise the God who saves me!"* (Emphasis mine.)

I remember every step I took toward Jacob's grave. I was still in pain from the surgery and had cried so much that it was difficult to even walk. My husband was holding me up on one side and his grandfather held me on the other. Although I was afraid to face this storm and couldn't bear the thought of seeing our baby's casket, the Lord miraculously placed a shield around me and held me up lest I should stumble. He was my support and He took me to a safe place in Him. It was a place I'd never been before. It was a place called grace; God's sustaining grace. Although, there was sadness and darkness around me, He was the light that helped me walk each step of the way.

The following lyrics are from a song the Lord gave me in August of 2014. The words and melody came so quickly. It is a reflection of what the Lord has done for me in the midst of my storm. He longs to embrace you as well and wants to help you in your time of need.

I Am Safe

(copyright 2014)

Battered by the raging storms within
Washed up by the waves of pain

Wondering how to live
Would this storm ever have an end?
Drifting in a sea of doubt
I felt like there was no way out
I couldn't see the sun for all the clouds
Then I heard a voice from Heaven
Jesus was calling out my name
His hand reached out to rescue me
Now I'm finally safe!

Refrain

I am safe
When the storms of life are raging
I am safe
I am strong
Cause He gives me the strength to carry on
Rescued by His warm embrace
Resting in His grip of grace
I am safe

Verse

It was hard to see Him in the dark and storm
My vision blurred by all the pain
My vessel tossed and torn
Would this rainy season have an end?
Would my soul find peace in turmoil?
Would He rescue me in time?
I wondered if the sun would shine again
Then a light broke through the darkness
He was calling out my name
His hand reached out to rescue me
Now I'm finally safe

Bridge

Though He may not choose to calm the storms
upon life's raging sea
He is more than able to calm the storm in me—in me.

Yes, He kept me safe in the midst of my storm that day and continues to, as I rest in Him. We had a beautiful grave-side service. The sun was shining and the words that our pastor spoke were beams of hope that seemed to reach down into the depths of our broken hearts. He talked about Heaven and emphasized the fact that it was a real place. He reminded us that there is more beyond this life and the promise we have to see Jacob again one day.

My husband also addressed the gathering of our family and friends. He said, "I want everyone to know that Cindy and I are not angry at God, and we know that Jacob is being cared for by his Heavenly Father. We had big plans for him, and we were preparing a home for him. But the home he's in now is far greater than what we could ever provide for him. He is getting a lot better care than we could give him. This life is but a vapor and is so temporary. We need to focus on what eternity will be like and keep fighting the good fight of faith. The best is yet to come."

After the funeral my husband and I stood over Jacob's casket and said our goodbyes again. There would be several more hurdles to cross. But God would help me get over each of them one day at a time. It was by no means an easy part of the journey, but the Lord gave me the strength I needed as I focused on Him. However, I must say it was difficult to stay focused at times. As I look back I can see how He carried me through the pain.

A few weeks after Jacob's funeral, I had pretty much reached bottom again and couldn't see my way out of my pit of darkness. My husband didn't know what to do for me but pray and try to encourage me with God's Word.

The doctors had given me medication for an infection that I had developed because of the fact that I had become engorged. I was lactating and had no baby to breast-feed. I woke up one night hallucinating. It was as if the enemy himself was creeping around my room. I will never forget it.

I finally woke my husband and he began to pray and plead the blood of Jesus. He quoted Scripture from memory that I had never heard him quote before! He told me later that he knew that the spirit of God brought those Scriptures to his mind. We could feel the presence of the Lord as He interceded on my behalf. It wasn't long before I drifted off into a peaceful sleep.

Satan will try to set up residence in your mind when you are at your weakest. I am convinced that he will creep in any way he can, even if it's through medications. He will tell you that there is no use trying and make you feel like giving up. He will tell you these lies for as long as you will listen. I am glad to report to you that there is a way out of that darkness. There is power in prayer; there is power in God's Word, and there is power in the name of Jesus!

Hebrews 4:12

For the word of God is quick, and powerful, and sharper than any twoedged sword, piercing even to the dividing asunder of soul and spirit, and of the joints and marrow, and is a discerner of the thoughts and intents of the heart.

Power in Prayer ...

I had many people holding me up in prayer during my storm. There were times I couldn't pray for myself, and my friends and family were standing in the gap for me. They would wrap their arms around me and say two simple words, "I'm praying." That was like music to my ears! I knew that was what I needed most. When you have people praying for you that is worth more than money can buy.

The Bible tells us that the effectual fervent prayer of a righteous man availeth much. Satan knows this and will try his very best to stifle your prayers in your time of weakness. If you can't pray for yourself, don't hesitate to reach out to others that will be willing to pray you through to brighter days.

I specifically recall a special pastor friend of ours that prayed for us. He knew that I had been in the hospital, but had not heard the outcome. He called Anthony the day after I came home from the hospital. He and his wife had also experienced the loss of a child and felt our pain as Anthony shared the news of Jacob's passing. He prayed with Anthony, asking God to strengthen and comfort our hearts. As he was praying Anthony lifted his right hand up toward Heaven. He said that what he experienced that night was like nothing he had ever felt before. As he held his hand up in faith, he felt a gentle embrace. It was as if the Lord had taken hold of his hand and lifted it up a little higher.

Anthony knew he had been touched by the Master's hand, and he knew that God was going to give him strength for the days ahead in order to help me through the storm. He wasn't worried about himself. He was worried about how he would handle me. He knew how fragile I was and how difficult the days ahead would be for me. *He knew I was learning for the first time in my life how to weather the storm and how to reach for God's hand in the dark.*

The following letter is from this pastor. I would like to share in hopes that it will bring comfort to your heart, as it has mine.

5/11/04

Dearest Cindy and Anthony,

I have set out to record a few words as a stimulus to your faith. It is with humble appreciation for your experience that I remind you of a few things. I know that you already know these truths, but NOW I know you KNOW.

Last fall, before anyone knew of God's plan, He chose to create a new soul for His eternal universe. This creation became incarnate in human flesh through your love for each other in the form of Jacob Anthony. Because His ways are not our ways, and His thoughts are not always our thoughts (Isa. 55:8), circumstances occurred which we may never understand this side of Heaven.

But, I want you to always remember, that regardless of what happened to your family, be assured that the Lord never makes a mistake. You named this child, and he is an eternal child of God. God breathed into him the breath of life (though only for an earthly day), and he became a living soul. The Bible says, *"But, beloved, be not ignorant of this one thing, that one day is with the Lord as a thousand years, and a thousand years as one day"* (II Peter 3:8). You got to hold him for the better part of one thousand years!

I cannot begin to imagine what you all have experienced, but I do know this one thing. I am a father, twice, and there is never enough time to hold them close and love them, never even in a million years. Time is so fleeting. You gave him your very best while you carried him and in the few hours both of you had to actually hold him. God never requires more than that of anyone, not even His only Begotten son. You do your best, and God does the rest. Why He chose his path, is not for us to question, as long as we have been faithful to follow the path He has chosen for us.

Cindy, you are a mother, who has experienced her first Mother's Day, not as any mother would have chosen, but as God has chosen. Anthony, next month, you will face Father's Day, as a father for the first time, but you have not lost your child, Jacob. He is personally being cared for by your Heavenly Father. What could be better than being submitted to that reality? Not of your choosing, but of His!

Our prayers continue every day, for the both of you. When we are privileged to be in your presence again, we will speak of these things, and cry together, and praise God together for His gracious love and wisdom. WE love you as our own children, and know that your faith is being stretched and exercised. Remember to read of God's comfort and its purpose in your lives at this time (II Cor. 1:3-7).

The adverse winds blew against my life. My little ship with grief was tossed. My plans were gone— heart full of strife and all my hopes seemed to be lost—"Then He Arose" on word of peace. "There Was A Calm"—a sweet release.

A tempest great of doubt and fear possessed my mind; no light was there to guide, or make my vision clear. Dark night! 'Twas more than I could bear; "Then He arose", I saw His face; "There was a calm"—filled with His grace.

My heart was sinking 'neath the wave of deepening test and raging grief; All seemed lost, and none could save, and nothing could bring to me relief—"Then He arose"—and spoke one word, "There was a calm"—IT IS THE LORD"!

—selected

Because of Calvary,
Dr. Wade

Journal writing October 2014 ...

Resting in the shadow of His wings.

Trusting He knows best.

He knows all things.

I'm abiding in the secret place of the most high;

While I'm resting in the shadow of His wings

Weathering the Storm

While we are weathering the storms of life, we must keep our eyes on Jesus and listen for His voice. When we entertain negative thoughts from those around us or from Satan himself, we will find ourselves sinking beneath the waves of doubt and fear again.

When you are in the midst of a storm, one of the most important things to do is surround yourself with strong Christians. You need people that will hold you up in prayer and that will encourage you to bury yourself in God's Word and not bury yourself in your pain.

Remember, God's Word is a lamp unto our feet and a light unto our path. He knew there would be times of despair and darkness, so He gave us His infallible Word to stand on. When there's darkness all around you and you don't reinforce positive Christian principles, you will drown in a sea of misery.

As we look at a familiar story in the Bible when Peter was in the midst of a storm and took his eyes off of Jesus, we learn that he began to sink. But, as soon as he focused his eyes on Jesus, He was safe! He was able to rise above the storm because he reached out for his life-line.

We, too, have to stay focused on the Master, and if we do, we will make it through any storm that comes our way. Keep holding on, and never give in to negativity! Jesus is your lifeline, so look for Him and you will find Him reaching with outstretched arms ready to embrace you in your storm!

Firmly Planted ...

Consider the flowers of the field. The rains have made them grow into something beautiful. They seem fragile, and we wonder how they weather the storms without being blown away. The winds toss them about; the heavy rains seem to drown them, and yet after the storm is over, these colorful creations stand tall. How does that happen? Their roots are firmly planted. The rains actually make them stronger. Plants grow the most during fierce winds. The roots reach far down into the ground, being nourished by minerals in the soil and the water, making them strong enough to weather the storms.

Strong roots make healthy plants. And in the life of a Christian, strong roots make strong Christians. God wants to "grow" us spiritually, and in order for that to happen, it takes the rain. We need the Living Water, and we need our sustenance, the minerals of the Word of God. When the storms come our way, He's growing us and challenging us to reach way down into the depths of our souls, tapping into the faith and hope that is available in order for us to weather the storms! If we are firmly planted in Christ Jesus, we can withstand the winds and storms that come.

So keep looking for Him in the darkness, and you will find Him. The waves may be tossing, and winds may blow, but you will find Him in the midst. Listen for His still small voice and He will speak peace to you. *"My ears have heard of you before, but now my eyes have seen you"* Job 42:5. Job saw God in the storm and that was enough for him. And it is enough for you and me!

If we never experience the storms, we will never experience who He really is. I thought I knew the Lord before the storm, but not like I know Him now. I know Him as my fortress, my deliverer, my comforter, and my ever present help in time of trouble. He is a personal Savior, and I'm so glad I know Him and that He knows my name (Matthew 10:30-31).

Needing Him is the key to knowing Him.
Sarah Young - Jesus Calling

Chapter 8

Bitter or Better?

In the midst of my healing process, my doctor decided that I should try going to a support group. I reluctantly agreed to go and convinced my husband to join me. He wasn't too sure about going to this because he was afraid that it would pull me down and have a negative effect on me.

We attended our first group session and determined very quickly that it was not a Christian support group. As the attendees shared their stories, they spoke as if they had no hope. Some spoke of suicide, and none spoke with any faith in the Lord.

There was one woman in particular that stood out among the rest. Her precious baby died four years prior because her babysitter overdosed her with Benadryl. This poor mother was carrying so much bitterness and grief. It was an eye opener for me because I didn't want to walk down that same road and be in a state of depression for years to come.

It was our turn to share our story. As my husband talked about his faith in Christ and how we weren't angry at God, you could have heard a pin drop. He shared with these women that he wanted to be like Job in the Bible, like Paul, and like other heroes of the faith. He told them what Job had gone through and how he trusted God in spite of his trials. He told them about God's promises of seeing our loved ones again and how temporary our life is on earth. He urged them to find their faith.

After he finished, a woman spoke up and said, "Yeah, but we aren't Paul, and we aren't Job." My husband's reply was, "I know, but I want to be like them and pattern my life according to what the Bible says. They were people just like us, and when their faith was tested, they passed with flying colors. If they could make it after all they had been through, I know I can make it. We can't give up. We have to press toward the mark of the high calling which is in Christ Jesus; forgetting those things which are behind. No one is exempt from pain."

The counselor said nothing. She offered no hope to anyone. She only sat there and listened to these women roll around in self-pity and bitterness. I could see very plainly that these women were getting nowhere in their healing process. They had been coming to these sessions for over three years and had not gotten any better. They were still holding on to bitterness! They had buried their hope in the rubble of their brokenness!

It was very sad, and it made me very grateful for my Christian heritage. It also made me realize that I wasn't as bad off as I might have thought. I had faith to hold on to! I just had to make the choice to hold on to faith instead of bitterness! I had to put into practice everything that I had learned about God's promises. It was time for me to claim them for myself and time for me to stand up for what I really believed. I knew that if I didn't make the right choice, I might travel down a path of bitterness. I had to make the choice to turn around and get past the past! I had to turn the page, but that would take some time.

The question has been asked before, "What do the people who don't know the Lord do?" Well, we see what they do. Most of them stay in a state of depression and never let go of the past. Many times they bury their hurt by drinking alcohol or turning to drugs, which makes a bigger mess of their lives. They go on living hopelessly defeated by their past hurts.

I am so thankful that we can turn to Jesus! He is our hope, and He is the healer of broken hearts (Psalms 147). He can touch places in our hearts that no therapist or counselor can ever reach. All it takes is just one touch of His hand. It is a supernatural healing that can take place in our lives as we look to Him. It is a powerful touch! It is a miraculous intervention, and it is available for you.

Remember that Jesus is our ultimate counselor. Isaiah 9:6 says, "*His name shall be called Wonderful, Counsellor, The mighty God, The Prince of Peace.*" He always has an ear to listen at any time. Psalm 40:1 says, "*I waited patiently for the Lord; and he inclined unto me, and heard my cry.*"

You don't have to live in the pit of despair. Psalm 18 says, "*He reached down and drew me out of a horrible pit.*" Reach out to Him, and He will meet you where you are. Allow your hope to be resurrected!

I am glad to say that the final time that we attended the grief session, the counselor asked my husband to pray at the end. She said, "We have never done this before, but I would like to ask you to pray for us as we dismiss our meeting tonight."

What a privilege it was to have the opportunity to pray for those hurting women. God placed us there for a reason and used our situation to help others in need and to help guide them towards their healing.

Blessed be God, even the Father of our Lord Jesus Christ, the Father of mercies, and the God of all comfort; Who comforteth us in all our tribulation, that we may be able to comfort them which are in any trouble, by the comfort wherewith we ourselves are comforted of God (2 Corinthians 1:3-4).

As you turn your eyes upon Jesus and make the choice to be better and not bitter, may the Lord bring restoration to your brokenness, so you can begin to live again. Your heart will continue to wither, and your hurt will only multiply if you remain in a bitter state. It will continue to take the joy out of living and will rob you of the blessings God has in store for you. For your sake and the sake of your family, don't allow Satan to overcome you with bitterness. Remember you are an overcomer through Christ Jesus!

Chapter 9

Lord, It Hurts

I continued to struggle with the pain. I had good days and bad days. It was part of the healing process. Grief from the loss of a child is nothing you ever "get over"; it's something you get through with God's help. I could give you all the facts on what the books say about grief and what stages to expect, but we will all handle grief differently. I found that once I came to the place where I was ready to release my pain and grief to God, He could begin healing my broken heart, but not until then.

Many of us, including myself, have an extremely difficult time understanding why God would allow hurtful things to happen. I asked why many times, and received no answers. I was given some sound advice from a pastor when I asked her the "why" question. She told me something that will forever remain in my mind. She said that there are some things that we have to put up real high on a shelf and not bring down. It's like storing away a fragile vase. You know how delicate it is, and you put it in a special place where it won't get broken.

We can do the same thing with our unanswered questions. The questions themselves aren't fragile; however, we are. And if we continue to fill our minds with these unanswered questions, we will soon "break." The point being, when we keep taking them "off the shelf" we only become distraught again. We have to leave them with the Lord. The Bible says for us to take our burdens to the Lord and leave them with Him.

Matthew 11:28-30

Come unto me, all ye that labor and are heavy laden, and I will give you rest. Take my yoke upon you, and learn of me; for I am meek and lowly in heart: and ye shall find rest unto your souls. For my yoke is easy, and my burden is light.

When you have questions and you are having a hard time making sense of everything, I encourage you to express your feelings. Cry out to God and reach out to your church family as you seek godly counsel. You may even want to journal your feelings or your prayers. It has proven to be therapeutic for me in many ways. In the following journal, I expressed my feelings about how much I missed Jacob:

Journal writing 6/28/04 ...

I miss Jacob so much. I long to hold him in my arms. I don't understand why God allowed this to happen, but I will continue to serve the Lord and trust that He knows best. (I was trying to put my faith into practice.)

I love my little Jacob. All of his kicks would come in the early morning hours before I got out of bed. I long to hear his heart beat strongly on the monitor at the hospital. I so looked forward to taking him home with us and getting to know his personality.

My arms are empty. The house feels so empty. There is a sadness that lingers within the walls which reflects the inside of my heart. Lord, somehow, some way, fill the walls of this house with laughter and joy.

Jesus, please give Jacob a kiss for me today. Hold him up close in your arms and tell him that Mommy and Daddy love him so much.

Jacob, Mommy is determined to see you in Heaven one day! Until then, your daddy and I will continue to work for Jesus and tell of His saving power. I miss you so much. I sure would like to kiss the back of your cute little neck. I should have kissed it more, but I was afraid of making you uncomfortable with all the cords you had wrapped around you. You were such a perfect baby. Your hands and feet were so pretty. Look for your Mommy and Daddy in Heaven one day. We'll get to spend eternity with you! We'll be there when God is ready for us, and our work is finished down here!

God understands, and is compassionate and long-suffering toward a hurting heart. With most wounds there's usually a scar. Psalms 147 says, *"He heals the broken hearted and binds up their wounds."* That doesn't mean that you won't cry anymore. You will still have times of grieving. And that is normal and natural. Your heart will be changed forever. You will never be the same. However, I believe the scar is there to remind us from where God has brought us. Just look at the example of Jesus. He's carried us all the way from the cross, and He has the scars to prove it. May your scars be a reminder of from where God has brought you and where He will continue to lead you.

It was September 3rd, just four short months since our Jacob went to be with Jesus. I had decided to go to the cemetery on the spur of the moment. I thought I would just go and talk some things out with the Lord. I still needed to work through some things in my heart concerning the whole situation. These are the words that the Lord inspired me to write in my journal when I returned home that day:

Journal Entry September 3, 2004

I went to Jacob's grave today around 4:30. The sun was shining. The winds were blowing, and the birds were singing. It was as if God himself was breathing His peace upon my aching heart. The beautiful oak trees stood tall and strong, reminding me of God's strength and His infinite power. I could hear a melody in my heart: "His Eye is On the Sparrow and I know He watches me." Slowly, He was making all things new again for me, reminding me that His eye was on Jacob just as it is on me even now. I take comfort in knowing that there is not a sparrow that falls to the ground that He is not mindful of.

Jesus knows what it feels like to have a heavy heart. He even knows what it feels like to have the weight of the sins of the world on His shoulders. He knows what pain feels like, for He suffered it all on the cross of Calvary for my sake. He did it all for me. He bore my sin, my grief, my pain on the cross. Oh, that I may know Him in the power of His resurrection and in the fellowship of His sufferings, being conformed unto His death.

Must Jesus bear the cross alone and all the world go free? No, there's a cross for everyone and there's a cross for me.

Lord, may this situation bring me closer to you. I realize that the trials of this life are nothing compared to what you have suffered for me. I know it takes the storm sometimes to change our perspective and to change our direction toward a life of consecration. I surrender all, and I will trust and obey you just like the old hymn says. Now, I can see why that hymn seemed to leap off the page a few months before Jacob was born. I learned to play it on the piano, and now I am learning to live it like I mean it!

Help me to trust you and do whatever it is that you want me to do. I want to live for you and be a true testimony and witness for your Glory and your Honor. Anoint me to be effective in ministry as I daily take up my cross and follow you! I will serve you. Hebrew 10:23 says, *"Let us hold fast the confession of our faith (HOPE) without wavering, for He who has promised is faithful."*

I will hold to God's unchanging hand in the midst of uncertainty and have determined in my heart to cling to what I know to be true. I will trust and believe that GOD IS FAITHFUL! Use Me Lord!

Trust and Obey

by John H. Sammis 1887

When we walk with the Lord in the light of His Word,
What a glory He sheds on our way;
While we do His good will, He abides with us still
And with all who will trust and obey.

Not a shadow can rise, not a cloud in the skies,
But His smile quickly drives it away;
Not a doubt or a fear, not a sigh or a tear,
Can abide while we trust and obey.

Not a burden we bear, not a sorrow we share,
But our toil He doth richly repay;
Not a grief or a loss, not a frown or a cross,
But is blessed if we trust and obey.

But we never can prove the delights of His love
Until all on the altar we lay;
For the favor He shows, for the joy He bestows,
Are for them who will trust and obey.

Then in fellowship sweet we will sit at His feet.
Or we'll walk by His side in the way.
What He says we will do, where He sends we will go;
Never fear, only trust and obey.

Refrain

Trust and obey, for there's no other way
To be happy in Jesus, but to trust and obey.

"Lord Almighty, blessed is the man who trusts in You."
Psalm 84:11-12

Jesus Loves Me?

I seemed to be getting stronger emotionally. Then a whirlwind came. It caused me to plummet into a stage of bitterness and shock. I found out that a close family member was expecting and had not "planned" the pregnancy. I could not imagine having to face the situation because it would be another reminder that my arms were empty. To make it an even more trying situation, I found out that the baby's due date was on Jacob's one year birthday.

I would have to walk that same corridor in the hospital one year later. How was I going to do that? In my mind, it seemed impossible.

I had decided that I was giving up! I was not going to church on this particular Sunday, and that was highly unusual. I was certain that God didn't love me! I remember telling my mom that I felt like God was slapping me in the face. Oh, how untrue that was! This baby would prove to be a blessing to our family.

As my husband got ready for church, he "preached" a sermon to me. He was so good at that. His sermon this time was about Job and all that he had been through. He pleaded with me not to give up, reminding me that brighter days were ahead. However, he was getting nowhere with me. Mentally, I had blocked him out and felt like telling him, "Talk to the hand."

Besides, he didn't know how I felt. He had not carried our son or given birth to him. He didn't understand. Regardless of whether he understood my feelings or not, everything he was saying was right. In my heart, I knew I needed to hear every word he spoke. I just didn't want to hear it from him.

He left for church, and I received a call from my mother. She came over and sat with me that morning. I remember telling her that I felt like God did not love me and that I was tired of trying to be strong.

Looking back I realize that I could not feel God's love because I had pushed Him away. I was too bitter to feel anything but hurt and anger. I had gone back to bed to try to sleep away my hurt, and I remember lying there telling God that if He would just have someone from church call me to encourage me (perhaps the preacher's wife), that would prove He was concerned about me. Well, the pastor's wife didn't call, but someone else did.

My husband's aunt called me and told me that she had been awake all night and felt a strong burden for me. She had no way of knowing my frame of mind, nor the things Anthony had told me that morning. However, she began to tell me almost verbatim all the things that my husband had said before he left for church. God had my number!

She reminded me that God is faithful and that brighter days were coming, just as my husband tried to tell me. She, too, begged me not to give up and urged me to keep on going, and she said to remember Job and all that he had gone through.

The Bible says that Job was an upright man without sin. This shows us that no one is exempt from trials. The Bible says that it rains on the just and the unjust. No matter how pure your life is before the Lord, you will suffer persecution. However, the rewards are great and the blessings are numerous. Just look at Job's life in the end.

The devil wanted the opportunity to test Job's faith and see if this righteous man would still worship God under difficult circumstances. A conversation took place between Satan and the Lord. Satan was convinced that Job only trusted God because of his comfortable life. God allowed Satan to bring disaster upon Job by taking away his health, his wealth, and his family; however, he told Satan not to touch his life (Job 1:12).

After everything was gone, Job said, *"Though He slay me, yet will I trust him."* (Job 13:14-16). Job passed the test, and his health and his wealth was restored. Once again Job's lap was filled with children, and grandchildren, and great grandchildren for four generations.

I have often heard my husband's grandfather say, "God has the devil on a leash, and he'll go as far as God allows Him." Job's life was proof of that.

We have to remember that God never promised us that we would not suffer in this life. If you are living and breathing, you will suffer hardships. Nothing will be perfect until we get to Heaven. With that said, we must realize that the devil himself wants to destroy us and make us believe that Jesus doesn't care when trials come our way. It is important for us to realize how much He really does love us and that we not turn away from Him.

Why is that important? What can God's love do? It can tear down walls of bitterness. It can break strongholds of depression and bring healing and restoration to broken hearts. That is why Satan wants to blind us and make us think that God doesn't love us. God's Word tells us that perfect love casts out all fear! God's love is a powerful gift. May you receive this gift fresh and anew today and experience His love in a way like never before!

"*Suffering is the occasion for experiencing the compassion of God*" (unknown).

Chapter 11

Jesus Loves Me This I Know!

As I continued to try and reason everything out, I found myself still asking the same question, "If God really loved me, why didn't He heal Jacob?" I had waited so long for this child and felt he was the miracle I had been praying for. So, why did He take him so soon? Was this how my Heavenly father showed His love for me?

It was hard to see past the pain, and the devil still tried to convince me that God surely must not love me. However, I knew deep down in my heart that this was not true. We can see a true picture of what God's love looks like when we look at the cross of Calvary.

Let's think for a moment of the suffering that Jesus went through, and keep in mind it was all for us! He was beaten and bruised and not even guilty as charged. The Roman soldiers spat upon Him, plucked His beard, pierced His side, and drove nails in His hands and feet all because there needed to be a sacrifice for our sins. Because of what He did on Calvary's cross, the price for our sins has been paid in full. No one else has ever shown this kind of love for us.

How could we ever doubt His love? If He never answered another prayer for us or ever met our needs again, we should realize His unfailing love for us. Even with this realization, it remains difficult, and it is easy for us to be blinded from the fact that He is weeping for us and with us!

Hebrews 4:15

For we have not an high priest which cannot be touched with the feeling of our infirmities; but was in all points tempted like as we are, yet without sin.

When we are experiencing grief, it's hard to put everything into perspective and realize God's love for us. It seems like we are holding on by a thread and hoping not to lose our grip.

I can remember how the Lord reminded me of His love for me one Sunday morning while I sat in church. I never dreamed that a song that I sang as a child would play such a big part in it. It was also the song that I sang to Jacob before he was ushered into the splendors of Heaven. The following journal explains.

July 2004

The Divine Appointment – Jesus does love me!

The sermon this morning was just what I needed. The pastor spoke about how God can restore our joy and put a praise on our lips even in our darkest hour. His text was out of Isaiah 6.

At the end of the service he said, "I feel like we need to sing 'Jesus Loves Me.' I know that is a little unusual, but I still feel we should sing it." As I stood at the altar, the words of that song melted my heart. I felt God's love pour over my heart like a balm or salve on my wound. The Lord used the song that I sang to my baby to touch my heart in a very special way. I was assured once again of God's undying love for me.

Jesus loves me this I know
For the Bible tells me so.
Little ones to Him belong.
They are weak but He is strong.
Yes, Jesus loves me.
The Bible tells me so.

(Written in 1860 as a poem by Anna B. Warner and included as part of a story meant to comfort the heart of a dying child.)

2 Corinthians 12:9

And he said unto me, my grace is sufficient for thee: for my strength is made perfect in weakness. Most gladly therefore will I rather glory in my infirmities, that the power of Christ may rest upon me.

Romans 8:38-39 says:

And I am convinced that nothing can ever separate us from the love of God. Neither death nor life, neither angels nor demons, neither our fears for today nor our worries about tomorrow – not even the powers of hell can separate us from God's love. No power in the sky above or in the earth below – indeed, nothing in all creation will ever be able to separate us from the love of God that is revealed in Christ Jesus our Lord (NLT).

Journal 9/16/04

Do not fear or be afraid! Remember what God's Word said. His eye is on the sparrow. If He knows when a sparrow falls to the ground, then how much more He is concerned about us. He loves us and every detail in our lives. He loves me – He loves me – Yes, Jesus loves me the Bible tells me so.

Matthew 10:29-31: *"Are not two sparrows sold for a penny and not one of them falls to the ground apart from the Father's will? But every hair of your head is numbered. Do not fear for you are more valuable than many sparrows."*

We matter to Him along with every detail in our lives. Your pain does not go unnoticed by Him. There is not a tear that you have cried that He is not aware of. He is for you, not against you. So please don't turn Him away in your desperation. Run to Him! He loves you!

Isaiah 53:3-5 (KJV)

He is despised and rejected of men; a man of sorrows, and acquainted with grief: and we hid as it were our faces from him; he was despised, and we esteemed him not. Surely he hath borne our griefs, and carried our sorrows: yet we did esteem him stricken, smitten of God, and afflicted. But he was wounded for our transgressions; he was bruised for our iniquities: the chastisement of our peace was upon him; and with his stripes we are healed.

Ephesians 3:17-19 (NLT)

Then Christ will make His home in your hearts as you trust in him. Your roots will grow down into God's love and keep you strong. And may you have the power to understand, as all God's people should, how wide, how long, how high, and how deep his love is. May you experience the love of Christ, though it is too great to understand fully. Then you will be made complete with all the fullness of life and power that comes from God.

More Scriptures on God's love:
John 4:7-21
1 John 4:8
1 John 4:16

Journal writing April 2013 ...
Lest I forget the wonder of the cross.
Lest I forget how Jesus paid the cost.
May Calvary remain alive in me;
And may Jesus Christ be glorified through me.

Climbing Up the Mountain

Although, I knew Jesus loved me, I felt like I was climbing the tallest mountain in my life. In reality, it was a mountain that eventually turned into depression. Some days I was strong and felt like I could climb. Other days I felt weak and stayed in the valley of gloom and despair until someone prayed and pulled me back out.

How was I ever going to make it to the top to see a ray of sunshine? On the days I felt weak, I certainly didn't feel like putting my hiking boots on! I was tired of trying to climb. I felt defeated.

Satan will distract you and try his very best to destroy you while you are trying to climb your way out of the valley. Remember the Scripture that says, *"Be sober, be vigilant, because your adversary the devil as a roaring lion, walketh about, seeking whom he may devour."* 1 Peter 5:8. This Scripture tells us that we must be aware of the snares of the devil. We have to fight, and we have to keep climbing. Satan's full time job in our lives is to distract us and bury us in our yesterdays! We must remember to keep our eyes toward our eternal goal which is Heaven.

Yes, Heaven is our eternal goal and our final destination as Christians. We must fight and equip ourselves in order to run this race and persevere no matter what comes our way. It will be worth it in the end!

God has given us the tools to overcome the enemy of our soul. We can overcome the mountain of depression. I realize that we will be sad at times, and we will cry. But that is normal. God made us and made our emotions, so it is normal to express them and to feel them. It's part of the healing process.

I understand we all want a quick fix when we are in pain. I certainly remember wanting that for myself when the pain was so fresh. I wanted someone to wake me up from my nightmare. We all long for someone or something to relieve us from our misery. Sometimes we look in the wrong places.

On the visit to the doctor to have my stitches removed, she asked me how I was doing. She had tears in her eyes and seemed to feel my pain. She said, "You know I can give you something that will help you get through this," and proceeded to offer me medication. I refused, and I must say reluctantly so. However, the words that came out of my mouth were, "Me and the Lord can handle this. I will do it with God's help."

To be perfectly honest with you, I would have loved to accept her offer at that time. And if I hadn't had a very strong husband, I probably would have accepted the offer. I am thankful that I didn't for so many reasons.

I know that the medication would have masked my pain for as long as I continued to take it. I would have eventually had to face my circumstances and raw emotions at some point. This was the choice that my husband and I felt was right for me.

We all have "mountains" to face, and they are not easy. God never promised us that life would be easy. He told us we would suffer tribulation (John 16:36). But He did promise us that He would be there for us to strengthen us and help us.

So when you are climbing your mountain, however high it may be, just remember to keep your eyes on Jesus, and He will help you climb to the top. And when you get to the top, I can guarantee that the views will be worth the climb. Remember, mountain climbing makes us stronger. It's physically draining, and it's hard, but He carries us to new places that we've never been before. He sustains us!

Don't look back. Don't look down. You'll feel yourself slipping, and you'll lose your grip. Look to Him for the help and strength you need to climb your mountain!

Journal writing 9/15/04

Today was a better day. I am climbing back up the mountain. Somehow I fall back down into the valley. Then slowly I make my way back up to the sunlight again. It is a struggle. I know I have to yield myself 100% to God's plan and purpose for my life and be willing to do whatever He wants me to do. I know I must keep my eyes on Jesus and not look back, but stay focused on Him. I so want to be an encouragement to those who are hurting.

I just read my devotion today, "I Am Thine O Lord," in my *Amazing Grace* book. It said, "God must always have His rightful place on the throne of the heart." My prayer today is: "Consecrate me now to thy service Lord, by the power of grace divine. Let my soul look up with a steadfast hope and my will be lost in thine." There is that word again, the one I keep thinking about – consecrate. It means dedicated to a divine service. Could it be that the Lord is calling me to do something in ministry for Him? I know God that you hear me – you see me – and I know you will make a way for me as I yield, trust and obey! Help me to keep my eyes on you, so I can keep climbing.

Journal writing 9/17/04

Still I rise never to give up and never to give in against all odds! I have felt afraid to get back up again because I may fall again. But that's when we learn that God is our refuge. When we fall down, we will get hurt, but Jesus picks us up again and dusts off the dirt and says let's try again.

I remember learning how to ride my bike as a little girl. I started out with training wheels and learned that I could do it. Then I felt brave enough to try it without the training wheels. I got on and rode for a little while, but fell. I tried again and again and fell several more times until I got better at it. The falls became less frequent as I became more confident. But still, there were bumps in the road, and I would fall again. I had to keep trying.

It's the same way with life. We travel down the road of life knowing that there will be some bumps in the road and some unexpected detours. We feel confident as we experience the mountain tops, but when a valley comes we feel like giving up. We must remember that for every valley there's a mountain on the other side. So keep climbing up the rough places, and use them for leverage. If the mountain was smooth, you'd have nothing to climb on! So accept the rocks and rough spots and use them for leverage. They'll make you stronger and will help you reach the top of the mountain again.

Get back on your bike and keep riding down the path of life, and remember He's on the bike with you!

***If you don't let go, you can't fall off! ***
Jerry Moffat

Embrace the Valley ...

If we lived on the mountaintop all the time, we'd miss out on the sweet fragrance of the lilies that bloom in the valley and the aroma of God's comforting presence when you feel Him ever so near. We'd miss out on the tranquility of the still waters when He quiets our souls in the midst of turmoil. We'd never experience the lush green pastures when His gentle wind of peace sweeps across our souls. It's in the valley that God's love is engraved deep into our hearts – hearts that were once bound by bitterness from the long winter winds that blew against our lives.

Don't miss out on His breath of peace that can soothe your heart, making all things new for YOU. It's those "valley" moments that will change your life, your character, and your eternal perspective. Remember, that between every valley, there's a mountain. Oh, and don't forget to use the jagged places to help you climb. Use them as stepping stones to get to the top, remembering all the times that God has met with you and has heard your prayer.

***"He makes my feet like the feet of a deer, and
sets me on my high places."***
Psalm 18:33 NKJV

Since moving to the mountains, I can really appreciate this passage of Scripture. The mountains of Tennessee have plenty of deer. You can watch them dart up the side of a rugged mountain effortlessly. They make it look so easy to climb up the jagged places so quickly. A whitetail deer can run as fast as forty miles per hour and can leap fifteen to twenty feet!

How can these fragile creatures have such stamina? God designed them that way, and He is saying to us that He will make our feet like that of a deer. He will give us the strength and the stamina to climb the tallest mountains that we face! Keep climbing, and don't allow Satan to distract you!

Boot Camp 101

"We wrestle not against flesh and blood but against principalities, against powers, against the rulers of darkness of this world, against spiritual wickedness in high places" (Ephesians 6:12).

Now let's talk about how to fight! First of all, I am fragile. I am sensitive, and I was not born with an instinct to fight. However, in order to survive spiritually, we have to learn how to fight spiritually!

The sooner we realize that we are MORE than conquerors through Christ Jesus, the sooner we will want to fight. There is a boldness I found when I realized that I have the power the fight off the enemy of my soul (Luke 9:1). God gives us the spiritual boldness that we need.

I do not wish to give the devil credit for anything by talking about his tactics. However, I feel that we need to recognize what we are fighting against so that we will rise up and be bold.

As we mentioned in a previous chapter, we have a choice to go down a spiraling road of depression and not come back. Or we can choose to rise above the doubt and fear and walk in victory! As Christians, there is a place in Him that we can go where true victory is ours! It's a place that only Jesus Christ can lead us to as we depend on Him.

It's not just a mind-over-matter thing. Dwelling on positive things is great, but it takes more than that. It's a matter of the heart and allowing the power of the Holy Spirit to work in and through your life!

When feelings of discouragement and sadness try to grip the very core of your being, you can stand against them and realize that God is bigger than your hurts! Put God's Word into practice. Use it to stand on. Apply it to your heart and your situation. Allow God's spirit to flow through you to empower you on your life journey! *"It's not by might, but by my spirit, sayeth the Lord"!*

Psalm 27:1

The Lord is my light and my salvation; whom shall I fear? The Lord is the strength of my life; of whom shall I be afraid?

I can remember a specific time that Satan tried to rob me of my victory and peace. It was over four years after Jacob went to be with Jesus. I was praying one day as we were traveling home from a vacation. I remember thanking the Lord specifically for His peace and the victory that He had given me, when all of a sudden, I felt a wave of negative thoughts about Jacob's death flood my mind. Those same feelings of grief and despair came over me in an instant. I knew that this was not from God.

I recognized immediately that it was a trick of the enemy, and I was not about to let him win this one! I had come too far to turn back! As soon as I began calling on the name of Jesus and pleading His precious blood, those feelings left instantly! It was amazing. I was finally learning how to fight!

The Bible says in Isaiah 59:19, *"When the enemy shall come in like a flood, the Spirit of the Lord shall lift up a standard against him."* The enemy can't win if we use God's Word in combat! So gear up with His Word upon your lips and in your heart and keep fighting for victory! You can win!

I have finally reached a point in my life that when I feel the devil trying to rob me of my victory and my joy, I just get mad at him. I get so mad at the devil that I want to give him a black eye. I do that by quoting the Scriptures that God has given me and by testifying of God's goodness. Remember, we are overcomers by the word of our testimony.

I can remember my husband's grandfather preaching many times and hearing him say, "We need to have bulldog tenacity when it comes to fighting this fight of faith! Never let go of God, and never give in to the devil!" He'd say, "Quitters never win, and winners never quit."

There are spiritual blessings we can receive as children of God. God's power is very great for those who believe (Ephesians 1:19). And once we realize that it is the same power that God used to raise Christ from the dead, we will find a boldness and strength in us that we can use to climb the highest mountain and fight against the fiery darts that the enemy throws our way.

We have to FIGHT! The Bible says, *"Fight the good fight of faith, lay hold on eternal life"* (1 Timothy 6:12). In order for us to fight, we must put on the whole armor of God. Ephesians 6:13 tells us, *"Wherefore, take unto you* the whole armor of God, that ye may be able to withstand in the evil day, and having done all, to stand."

What is the whole armor of God? Our answer is found in Ephesians 6:14-17.

> *Stand therefore, having your loins girt about with truth and having on the breastplate of righteousness. Having your feet shod with the preparation of the gospel of peace. ABOVE ALL, taking the shield of faith, wherewith ye shall be able to quench the fiery darts of the wicked." And take the helmet of salvation, and the sword of the spirit, which is the Word of God.*

Our Battle Plan ...

Recognize—Resist—Retaliate

We must **RECOGNIZE** the enemy of our souls. When negative thoughts flood your mind you can be sure that those thoughts are not from God. Satan will try any angle he can to attempt to rob us of our joy—our victory—our strength. Remember, *the joy of the Lord is our strength* (Nehemiah 8:11). Don't allow the enemy to steal your joy. He will paralyze you spiritually if you allow him. Recognize his tactics.

When we are under attack, we must **"RESIST *the devil and he will flee*"** (James 4:7). Speak the name of Jesus, and the devil will flee. There is power in the name of Jesus. Demons tremble at the very mention of His name. Plead His precious blood! There really is power in the blood of Jesus – wonder working power!

RETALIATE—Don't give up! Claim your rights as a child of God. God has already prepared a way for you to live in victory and win, so be bold and fight! There really is victory in Jesus! Use God's Word and fight with your spiritual sword!

Journal writing 2/15/11

Don't give up. Don't give in. By God's grace I know that you're gonna win. Keep the faith! Keep on running this race! I know you'll make it if you keep the faith!

Take courage weary soldier!
The Lord thy God is with you!
Fear not, though the battle rages!
With Him you cannot lose.
And in the midst of trouble,
The Lord will see you through!

"*Your life is a spiritual battlefield which requires you to get rid of your flip flops and tighten up your boot strings. This is boot camp and it's time to fight and finish strong!*"
Pastor Randy Johnson

Chapter 14

All Things New

I thought I'd never laugh again, never "live" again, and never see the sun shine again. "Brighter days are coming," my husband would say over and over to me. All I knew was that my arms were empty, and those 16 years of waiting had turned into more waiting and more disappointment. How could He possibly make all things new again?

In my moments of fear and questioning God, there were many times He met with me. He would whisper things into my heart and mind assuring me of His presence. I can tell you that I would have never experienced those special encounters with the Lord if I hadn't traveled this part of my journey. I will cherish those moments forever.

I eventually found that He's still God and He's still good even in our night seasons.

A familiar Scripture is found in Ecclesiastes 3:1-4 (KJV). It says:

> *To everything there is a season, and a time to every purpose under the heaven: A time to be born, and a time to die; a time to plant, and a time to pluck up*

that which is planted; A time to kill, and a time to heal; a time to break down, and a time to build up; A time to weep, and a time to laugh; a time to mourn, and a time to dance.

In this life we do experience different seasons, and unfortunately there are night seasons. However, as Christians we can experience God's grace in those dark times. His grace truly amazes me as I continue to walk in it and because of it on a daily basis.

There are seasons of blessing, seasons of struggle, seasons of pain, and seasons where the rains are necessary in order for God to "grow" us. But we all wonder at some point in our lives how God can make all things new after tragedy hits. It's the grace of God that carries us from season to season.

As we learn to trust Him through each season, whether it's in the dead of winter spiritually speaking, in the midst of summer thunderstorms, or in the middle of springtime when everything is bright and beautiful and is going our way, He brings to us a new kind of grace that we have never experienced. He gives us a new kind of peace that we have never known, provides new victories, renews our minds, restores our brokenness, allows us to see things through spiritual eyes, and gives us an ambition and determination to make it whatever season we find ourselves in.

Summertime

Summertime can bring a lot of fun times with splashes in the pool and giggles from little ones on the playground, with cookouts, and times of fellowship with friends and family. It's easy to be happy and laugh when things are going our way and when the sun is shining bright. But even summer time can bring some hefty winds and thunderstorms, and then it's not as easy to smile.

It was the summer of 2004, a few months after Jacob passed away. Spring had come and gone, and things in my life were still dark and bleak. This darkness was only magnified by the series of hurricanes we had that year. It was one of the worst years ever for the state of Florida. We had four hurricanes that summer.

Large buildings were destroyed along with houses and roads. They all had to be rebuilt. Just like all the rebuilding that would have to take place in the cities that were affected, God was rebuilding me! I was under construction, and it wasn't a pretty sight. I was a "work in progress," and I still am! He was in the process of RENEWING me by His grace, RESTORING MY brokenness, and RESURRECTING my hope in Him! Thankfully, He was and still is patient with me.

You may be reading this thinking that things will never get better. Your grief has overtaken your spirit, but you will laugh again. And yes, you will even cry again. Seasons of life come and go, but whatever the season you find yourself in, you can rest in the fact that HE WILL SUSTAIN YOU BY HIS GRACE!

The following lyrics are from a song the Lord gave me in 2013. It encourages us to hold on to hope no matter what season we are in.

Hold On to Hope
by Cindy Johnson
(copyright 2013)

What's that I hear in the distance?
It's the song of the nightingale.
God made him to sing when the sun is not shining;
When the darkest of midnight prevails.
He sings such a beautiful melody;
Even when things aren't bright.
His song is one that reminds us,
Weeping only endures for the night.

Refrain:

So hold onto hope in the darkness
Sing your song of praise
It won't be long 'til the morning has broken
Bursting with the dawn of a new day!

What's that I hear in the distance?
It's the song of the morning dove.
She's singing for morning has broken;
Declaring a new day's begun.
Her melody echoes a message;
One day endless joy will come.
When the shadows of night will be lifted forever;
And we'll soar on the wings of His love!

What's that I hear in the distance?
Is that a trumpet sound I hear?
Could that be Gabriel preparing,
For the coming of Christ is near?

It won't be long 'til He calls us,
To our Heavenly home above.
Where the dawn of a new day's forever;
And we'll live in the light of His love!

Springtime

After a long cold winter with no leaves left on the trees and no sign of life in God's garden, we always welcome springtime. As the season changes, we eventually see new life bursting all around. God begins to gently brush the barren trees with signs of glorious shades of green. As warmer weather approaches, the flowers begin bursting with vibrant colors, and the birds begin to sing. Spring has finally sprung!

If you listen closely by a rippling brook, you can hear the rhythm of the river flowing in sync with the birds singing their symphony of praise, welcoming new life! It's a song they've been waiting to sing all winter.

Get ready to sing your song as He begins to birth new life into your withered soul. You'll feel the gentle breezes of God's peace sweep over your heart. Those cold winds that blew and sent a chill into the very core of your heart will fade, and the pain that used to seem unbearable will lessen. The dreary days of hopelessness will begin to fade, and you will feel His blanket of peace overshadow you.

As you begin to lean upon His everlasting arms, you will feel Him wrap His arms of strength around you, filling your heart with the warmth of His spirit; and you can rest, taking comfort underneath the shadow of His wings.

"The nightingale sings its most melodious
song in the night season."
Rev. Bert F. Ford

What if God took the song of the birds away? There would be such a void. Our lives sing a song.

Lord, help our life-songs not to be filled with sour notes, but with melodies of your grace that bring you glory.

God really does have a way of making all things new
again! Hold onto hope in your night season!
The dawn of a new day is on the horizon!
You will laugh again.
You will live again!
Keep looking up for your
ray of hope!

Chapter 15

God's Promise Fulfilled

It was November 18, 2004, and Thanksgiving was right around the corner. I was dreading the holidays and was tired of putting on a smile to go to work every day. That morning, one of my clients came by my office to tell me about a song she wanted me to hear. It was entitled, "Joy in the Morning." I told her that I knew the song and started singing a line of it: "Hold on my child; joy comes in the morning. Weeping only lasts for the night." As she tried to encourage me, she told me not to lose hope and that joy was just around the corner—was it ever!!!

I received a phone call from my husband before lunch. He said he needed to come by my office to talk to me about something. I immediately assumed someone had died and told him not to bother coming by if that was the case. I told him I couldn't handle any more grief.

He said, "I just need to talk to you, and I'll be there to meet you for lunch." He walked into my office and sat down at my desk showing me a picture of one of the most beautiful baby boys I had ever seen. Then he asked me this question, "Do you want to be this baby's Mommy?" I couldn't believe my ears!

The previous day, he had found out about this seven-week-old bundle of joy through a co-worker and had arranged to go and see him without my knowledge. He wanted to make sure things were going to work out before he told me about it. We contacted an attorney immediately, and the paperwork was completed in a few hours. We were able to bring our new baby boy home that night, and he has been with us ever since!

What a miracle and what a whirlwind! God had all of this planned from the beginning of time. He knew there would be an Isaac, and He had been preparing my heart for him for sixteen years. What if God had answered the prayer that I prayed so many times to take away my desire to have a child? Thank God for those unanswered prayers!

I believe He placed the desire to be a mother in me for a reason, and that was not only to be Jacob's mother, but to be Isaac's as well! God placed my husband at the right place, the right job, and at just the right time to fulfill this promise He had made to me years before. I have no way of knowing exactly what Isaac's medical due date was, but I have no doubt what God's due date was! His timing was perfect!

His promise was fulfilled at just the right time. No, it wasn't according to my time or my way, but it was God's way of showing me, as well as many others, that God is always working for our good and that He has a master plan. God moved mountains in order to accomplish His will for our lives as well as Isaac's! God is a mountain mover, so look to Him to move your mountain!

If you are still longing to be a mother, just remember that God has placed that desire in your heart for a reason. Continue to seek His perfect will for your life and ask Him to guide your every step on your journey to becoming the mother He intended you to be. He will open doors that no man can open. He will shut doors that no man can shut. So, if the doors shut, don't get too discouraged. It is God's way of saying, "It's not in my time."

Unexpected but Selected

God kept His promise! He sent us a beautiful baby boy, and it was in a way that we least expected, just as He said He would. I had been dreading the holidays and had given back all of the baby gifts we had received for Jacob. We had no bottles or baby clothes in the house! It was instant baby that day. Yes, in one day, we were holding our new baby boy. It wasn't like we planned, but how God planned it!

I will never forget the first time I saw Isaac. I felt like I was dreaming! I walked over to where he was sleeping and picked him up. I can't tell you how good it felt to hold this precious gift from God! We took him home that night, and our family greeted us with utter excitement. We could barely get in the door with him. I can't describe the joy that our entire family experienced as they each held our new baby boy. It was unbelievable! Our laughter and joy was finally in our arms! It was a miracle, and it had been quite a journey!

My husband and I named Isaac before we even knew him. It was just a few months after Jacob went to be with Jesus. We were lying in bed talking one night, and my husband asked me, "If we ever have another baby boy would you like to name him Isaac?" My reply was, "I can't even begin to think about that right now. Besides, it took 16 years for Jacob to come along, and I don't have 16 years to wait for another. But, if by some way of a miracle God sends us one, I guess the name Isaac would be fine."

Love at first sight
November 2004

I didn't think anything else about it until the day Isaac came along. Three months after we had that little talk, Isaac had come into our lives. We knew what his name would be.

One night, a few weeks after the Lord sent Isaac into our lives, I was rocking him in his bedroom. Suddenly, as I was praying and thanking God for His faithfulness, a thought occurred to me. The Lord reminded me what the name Isaac meant. It means God's promise fulfilled, and laughter, and joy! God had fulfilled His promise. He had literally filled the walls of our home and hearts with laughter and joy. That was an answer to a prayer that I had prayed shortly after Jacob died.

Hold on to the promise that God has given you. There are so many promises in God's Word. Cling to each one and stand tall with your head up high realizing that He knows your situation, and He is in control of all things and doeth all things well. He never makes a mistake!

Chapter 16

Praising Our Way Out of the Cave

There is no pit so deep that God's love is not deeper still.
Corrie ten Boom, survivor of the Holocaust

You might be asking the question, "How can I praise in the midst of my deepest pain?" How can I lift my hands to God when He has allowed this trial to come my way?" Well, I will tell you from experience that it was not easy for me. I wish I could tell you that both hands were lifted high to my Savior during my darkest trial. But, there were times in the very beginning of my healing process that I had no praise to offer Him. The shackles of grief and depression held my hands down low. I felt empty and defeated with nothing left to give but an ocean of tears.

God wants us to know that He understands our brokenness. He sees and understands our tears. However, He also wants us to see the power of praising Him in our valleys. Even the Psalmist David prayed and praised his way out of the cave of depression.

There is freedom and power when we praise God. There is something supernatural that takes place when we begin to praise and worship our Creator for who He is. Once we realize who God is and who He can be to us personally, we will see that He is all we need. He is enough to help us out of our cave of bondage.

He urges us to cry out to Him for help and has promised us that He would come to our rescue. However, our prayers must not only consist of requests, but praises as well. Psalm 100 says, *"Enter into his gates with thanksgiving and into His courts with praise. Be thankful unto Him, and bless His name."* He inhabits the praises of His people.

Praise brings us into His presence and that in turn brings the glory of the Lord. He will bring healing and restoration to our hearts. Once we enter into the Holy of Holies, we can experience glimpses of His glory – His divine presence.

Let's look at examples in God's Word of how He brings power and freedom to His people when praise begins.

Daniel prayed under pressure ...

Daniel, for instance, went from being the top advisor to King Nebuchadnezzar to receiving a possible death sentence by being thrown into a pit of hungry lions. As we read in Daniel 2, he takes a step in the right direction and began to bless the name of the Lord.

Daniel 2:20

Blessed be the name of God forever and forever, for wisdom and might are His. And He changes the times and seasons. He removes Kings and raises up kings. He gives wisdom to the wise and knowledge to those who have understanding. He reveals deep and secret things: He knows what is in the darkness and light dwells with him. I thank you and praise you, O God of my fathers.

Daniel chose to rise above his circumstances and turned to God for help. He praised Him! He acknowledged who God was! He recognized that He was with him and that He was his everything. He knew that God was in control. God's power was revealed when He answered Daniel's prayer by helping him interpret the king's dream. God protected him from the hungry lions! There is power in prayer and praise!

God's Word proves that He is all powerful! He can do anything! He has performed miracles time and time again. He created you and me and knows us better than anyone else can. He has even numbered the hairs on our heads (Luke 12:7).

Journal writing 9/13

He's no ordinary God. He's the Creator!
He made a dry highway in the middle of the Red Sea.
He used spittle when He healed the blind man.
He made man out of the dust of the ground.
He caused water to spew out of rock when Moses struck it.
He's no ordinary God!
He rolled back the Red Sea—not the way they thought it would be.
He told Naaman to dip in the Jordan, to cleanse him of his leprosy.
He turned water into wine!

He's no ordinary God! He's the Creator!

He will move in ways you least expect.

Don't put Him in a box. Remember, God's not human.

He is not bound by our rules and regulations.

His ways are so much higher than ours, we cannot comprehend them.

Skeptics ask why we should trust in the unseen. Well, I ask, "Why NOT trust Him?" His miracles are plain to see. Take a look at me! Take a look at all He's done for you recently!

When you can't see His hand, allow your faith to stretch BEYOND the unseen. Take a step of faith, and let God do the rest. As you are reaching for His grip, remember He's already holding you in the palm of His mighty hand. Trust in the one who knows you best, remembering that He's the one that loves you the most! He's highly capable of taking care of His own! After all, He IS God!

He is the Alpha, the Omega, the beginning and the end. He is our Wonderful Counselor, Mighty God, Everlasting Father, and the Prince of Peace. He is omnipotent. He is our Creator. I could expound endlessly on the greatness of God, but until we each experience Him for ourselves, we cannot grasp His awesomeness. How do we get to that place? We must enter into the throne room. How do we get there? We praise! We magnify! We worship Him for who He is!

Singing our way out of the pit …

Did I just say "sing" even in our night seasons of life? You might say, "First of all, I can't carry a tune in a bucket, so how can I sing if I wanted to?" Well, the Bible says to make a joyful noise unto the Lord (Psalm 100-1;2). It doesn't have to sound beautiful to you, but surely it sounds pleasing to our Heavenly Father when we worship Him from the depths of our hearts and bring the sacrifice of praise unto Him (Hebrews 13:15).

Sometimes it feels impossible to sing unto Him any kind of praise when our wounds are so deep. However, I have found that when I sing praises to Him even when I don't feel like it, He honors that.

There have been times when I couldn't pray, when the words wouldn't come. Sometimes I have an easier time "singing" a praise to Him. I have found that music can soothe an aching heart and can usher us into an attitude of worship.

Even King Saul was comforted by David's harp. When we keep our minds in an attitude of worship and fill our hearts and homes with music that is uplifting to God, it will change the atmosphere in our homes.

Philippians 4:8

Finally, brethren, whatsoever things are true, whatsoever things are honest, whatsoever things are just, whatsoever things are pure, whatsoever things are lovely, whatsoever things are of good report; if there be any virtue, and if there be any praise, think on these things.

David prayed his way out of the cave ...

The Psalmist David even praised his way out of the cave when he was running for his life (1 Samuel 23:14). Take note that he penned eight different Psalms while running from King Saul.

David shared his heart, and it is reflected as we read the book of Psalms. I believe that is why we can all relate to David so well.

He was a musician; he was good looking, and he seemed to have it all together on the surface. At times he was filled with discouragement and dealt with depression. Sometimes "the cave" even looked good to him.

We have all traveled a similar road. We have found ourselves running from our enemies; running from our fears and burying our deepest hurts and sometimes even our greatest treasures while silently suffering in our world of despair.

We have poured our hearts out to God. We've shared the good, the bad and the ugly with Him. We've questioned why and doubted that He was listening.

We can learn from David and pray and praise our way out of our cave!

Psalm 142a NIV Bible Gateway

The following is a contemplation prayer of David when he was in the cave of Abdola, which could be referred to as a prayer under pressure. This cave was a place of refuge, safety, a shelter, a peaceful place (*Jesus Calling Devotional Bible* p.893).

1
I cry aloud to the Lord;
I lift up my voice to the Lord for mercy.
2
I pour out before Him my complaint;
Before Him I tell my trouble.

3
When my spirit grows faint within me,
It is you who watch over my way.
In the path where I walk
People have hidden a snare for me.
4
Look and see, there is no one at my right hand;
No one is concerned for me.
I have no refuge;
No one cares for my life.
5
I cry to you, Lord;
I say, "You are my refuge,
My portion in the land of the living."
6
Listen to my cry,
for I am in desperate need;
rescue me from those who pursue me,
for they are too strong for me.
7
Set me free from my prison,
that I may praise your name.
Then the righteous will gather about me
because of your goodness to me.

At times David felt disoriented and defeated. He verbalized this in verses one and two. In verse three, he recognized God's presence. God knows how to bring us out of our cave of depression. In verse five David realized God's provision. He is our provider. Verse 7 says, "Bring me out that I may praise your name!"

Let's take a look at David's prayers in Psalm 57.

David prayed: *"Be merciful to me ... my soul trusts in you ... in the shadow of your wings I take refuge"* Psalm 57:1. He recognized God as his refuge and his protector.

Recognize Him as your provider of all you need! Run to Him!

He cried out to God for help. *"I will cry out to God Most High … who performs all things for me. He shall save me"* Psalm 57:2. Don't hesitate to cry out to God for help!

He sang in the cave! *"Be exalted, O God, above the Heavens; let your glory be above all the earth"* Psalm 57:5. Sing your way out of the cave!

In essence, we are all running for our lives just as David did. The enemy of our souls wishes to destroy us. David turned to God in his times of desperation and even encouraged himself in the Lord. I encourage you to do the same as you pray and sing your way out of the cave!

Paul & Silas praised and sang their way out of prison …

Another example of praising through difficult times is found in Acts 16:15-26. It's the story of Paul and Silas when they were persecuted and thrown into prison for preaching the gospel of Jesus Christ. They had been rent of their clothes and found themselves in a dark, damp cell.

The Scripture tells us that around midnight they prayed and began singing praises unto their God! Suddenly, there was an earthquake and the foundations of the prison were shaken. Immediately, the doors were opened, and everyone's bands were loosed!

I wonder what would have happened had they chosen to sit and complain about their situation instead of praising God in spite of it? They had every right to do so; however, they chose to call on God. They chose to praise

Him despite their gloomy circumstances. And because of their wise choice, their chains were loosed, and they were set free!

When we praise the Lord, our chains of bondage will be loosed! We too can be set free when we begin to praise the Lord! I can say from experience that there is freedom when we PRAISE Him through our pain.

Praise brings God's glory. God's glory brings His divine presence, and being in His presence brings full-ness of joy! The joy of the Lord brings the strength that we need in order to live a life of victory!

The following words are the lyrics to a song God gave to me as a result of my night season.

From Pain to Praise

Cindy Johnson
Copyright 2013)

I had nothing left to give—
No sacrifice of praise to offer up to Him
My dreams had all been shattered—
It seemed like there was just no hope in sight

But when the Spirit prayed for me—
He understood my plea
And in my helplessness—
I began to see.

Refrain
There is freedom when we praise
Him through our pain
Prison bars are loosed—
He takes the sting away
The more we love Him—
the more He sheds His light of grace;
To carry us from pain to praise.

In my time of brokenness—
He gave to me a song I'd never sung before
The melody was oh so sweet—
He whispered and He said, "I'm all you need."
When I was bound by grief and pain—
I called upon His precious name
Now I am free—
I sing my song of victory.

The following journal writing is one that reflects how God was turning my pain into praise. This was a few years after Isaac had come into our lives.

Journal writing 3/31/07
I visited Jacob's grave today, and as I stood there, the tears flowed silently as if someone had turned on a water faucet. The emptiness is still there as I reflect on the "kicks" in my belly that would come in the wee hours of the morning while I was carrying him.

It was amazing how I could feel such heartache, yet such a peace and calm assurance as I stood at the foot of Jacob's grave. The tears were flowing, but something felt different in my heart that day. I wasn't gazing over his grave with a heart full of questions as I usually did, and I wasn't leaving there worse off than when I came.

99

MY JOURNEY TO JOY

There was a praise coming out of my heart. It flowed thru the pain that I was feeling. The gratitude I felt in my heart began to swell from deep within. It was as if the Lord placed His garment of praise around me for the spirit of heaviness (Isaiah 61). Eventually, I felt as if chains of sadness were falling to the ground. The pain was beginning to fade.

As I looked across the cemetery thanking God for all that He has brought me thru, I gazed across the field, and my eyes fell upon Isaac and his daddy playing chase while running through the grave stones. It was a happy sight for sore eyes. Their laughter seemed to ring bells of joy thru the windows of my heart providing healing for my brokenness.

God is faithful! Bless the Lord O my soul and all that is within me; bless His holy name. He truly has done great things. Thank you Lord that you always give me grace for each moment and a song to sing in my midnight hour. Use me, Lord.

O death, where is thy sting? O grave, where is thy victory?
1 Corinthians 15:55

Chapter 17

The Power of Praise and Surrender

When the praises go up, God's glory comes down! When we spend time in His presence and begin to praise Him, our spirits are lifted. If your heart is heavy, praise is just the right medicine for you to experience true joy! The Bible says that He inhabits the praise of His people.

II Chronicles tells us about King Solomon carrying out the plans of his father David by building the temple in Jerusalem. He had to use the finest materials for God's house. He placed gold on the ceiling's beams, doorposts, walls, and doors. Even the nails that were used were made of gold.

Once the temple was completed, Solomon called for the elder leaders of Israel, the heads of the tribes, and the leaders of the families to come to him in Jerusalem. They praised the Lord with this song, "He is good; His love continues forever." Then the temple of the Lord was filled with a cloud. The priests could not continue their work because of it. The Lord's glory filled the Temple of God (II Chronicles 5:2-14). In the midst of our songs and praises, God's glory will come down!

Solomon prayed:

Please listen to my prayer and my request because I am your servant, Lord you are my God; hear this prayer your servant prays to you. Day and night, please watch over this temple where you have said you would be worshipped (II Chronicles 6:19).

In these Scriptures, we find some wonderful principles to follow in our daily walk with Christ. In the building of the temple, they only used the finest materials. As we come before the Lord in worship and praise, we should bring Him our best and our highest praise as well. Spending quality time with the Lord is essential to living a victorious life in Christ.

After the building was completed, they were ready to worship. The Israelites sacrificed so many sheep and bulls, there were too many to count. We, too, should bring our sacrifice of praise unto Him, bowing down before Him crying, "Holy, Holy, Holy, Lord God almighty!" He will honor our sacrifice of praise by filling us with His spirit and our hearts full of joy.

Notice Solomon's prayer. He pleaded with God to listen and recognized himself as God's servant. He surrendered his all to God. How many times have we stood to sing that familiar hymn of the church, "I Surrender All" and really meant it? I am guilty of singing it and not really meaning it with all my heart. It has taken me years to surrender my "WHOLE" heart to the Master.

As I have yielded to servanthood, my life has become filled with His peace. I can finally rest in the fact that my life is in His hands. I am confident that He will equip me with everything good in order to do His will (Hebrews 13:21).

Jeremiah 29:13 says, *"And ye shall seek me, and find me, when ye shall search for me with all your heart."* Notice the word "ALL." I never really paid much attention the latter part of that verse until the Lord led me down this path. Once I gave Him my "WHOLE" heart and said "Yes" to His will, I finally found the true peace and contentment I needed all along. It's all about submission because when we really surrender, we can experience fullness of joy in Him! When we experience the fullness and the reality of His power, we can be free! Free from what? Free from feelings of depression, fear, and freedom from ourselves.

You may be asking why we need to be free from ourselves. When we are constantly striving to please ourselves with what makes US happy, instead of striving to please God, we lose sight of the purpose that God has for our lives. When we rid ourselves of our own wants and desires, we will gain a heart of humility before Him. Be assured that kind of heart will not go unnoticed by Him.

II Chronicles 7:14

If my people who are called by my name will humble themselves, and pray and seek my face, and turn from their wicked ways, then I will hear from Heaven, and will forgive their sin and heal their land.

This Scripture was God's message to Solomon during the building of the temple of worship. Because of his willingness to serve, God manifested himself to Solomon.

When we willingly give to God full possession of our hearts and minds, His glory will be revealed in us and through us. He will fill a vessel that is willing to submit to him. If God's presence consumes us, we will have the power that we need to fight off the snares that Satan will throw our way!

Journal writing January 4, 2011

Another year has passed. It seems like such a blur, so many changes, but God in His sovereignty has worked everything for our good. God always makes good come from our trials. Romans 8:28 says, *"And we know that all things work together for good to them that love God, to them who are the called according to his purpose."*

Thank you, Lord, for your blessings on my family. I could never praise you enough. I cannot wait to bow down at your feet and praise you for all eternity! You have truly become my everything. I am determined this year to learn more of you and to hide your Word in my heart like never before. Give me wisdom and under-standing to know you more.

Fill my cup 'til it overflows with your goodness so that it may spill out to bless others. I know that if I don't spend quality time with you, I will miss out on blessings from the throne room that you long to give out.

This journey has proven to be a long one with twists and turns that were unexpected; however, I am thankful that you have walked with me every step of the way. You never gave up on me. You have revealed to me the true reason for living and that is to serve you and bring glory and honor to your name.

I am yours, Lord, your servant, ready to be used by you any way that you see fit. I love serving you. I love living for you. Blessings flow, grace is given and my joy is renewed as I give myself to you willingly. Use me, Lord

Total praise and surrender = God's greatest blessings!

Chapter 18

Bouncing Back

It is our faith in God that helps us bounce back after tragedy hits. It is our faith that carries us through our times of fear and pain. Our faith is what leads us away from our present state of hurt to a renewed mindset and healing that comes from God.

A few years ago, I had the privilege of praying with a woman on Easter Sunday. I asked her what I could help her pray about, and her reply was, "I'm just trying to find my faith." She had lived her life far away from God and had experienced a life full of pain, but she had finally come to the realization that what she needed was faith in order to bounce back.

Many times when my pain was so fresh, I wondered how I was ever going to bounce back. My faith was not as resilient as I would have liked it to be. I looked for books and testimonies of other women who went through a similar trial so that I could see how they made it. When looking for such books, there were not too many to choose from. The ones that I found only spoke of the sadness in their lives and NOT how they made it through victori-ously. I needed to see how they overcame their circumstances. Anyone can write about his or her sad story, but that's not what I needed to hear. I needed to hear how they overcame, how God turned their tragedies into triumph, and their tests into testimonies.

One day I came across a story in one of my devotionals about a remarkable writer named Fanny Crosby. Her story inspired me because she was a wonderful example of a woman of resilience and faith. Despite her circumstances, her life exemplified that of an overcomer.

She became blind at 18 months of age when a doctor treated her eyes improperly. Shortly after her blindness occurred, her father died, and she was raised by her mother and grandmother. At age five she was taken to the best eye specialist in the country. After examining her eyes, he said, "Poor child, I am afraid you will never see again." Surprisingly, Fanny did not think she was "poor." It was not the loss of sight that bothered her. It was the thought that she would never receive the education the other children had. She wrote, "Although I cannot see, I am resolved that in this world, contented I will be. How many blessings I enjoy that other people don't? To weep and sigh because I'm blind I cannot and I won't."

To make ends meet, her mother was very busy working, so it was her grandmother that became an unforgettable influence in her life. It was her grandmother that introduced Fanny to the Bible. She devoured the Scriptures and could repeat from memory the book of Proverbs, Song of Solomon, and much of the New Testament!

Near her 15th birthday, she received the news she could go to The Institute for the Blind in New York City. Fanny was so happy and cried, "O thank God. He has answered my prayer, just as I knew He would." She spent 23 years there with the first 12 as a student. She was a teacher for the remainder of that time. While teaching, she was inspired to write poetry.

By age 23, Fanny was the sightless guest of Congress. When she paid tribute to Congress, she delivered no pathetic story, but simply recited some poems about the tender care of a loving Savior. The notable assembly consisted of John Quincy Adams, Thomas E. Benton, and Jefferson Davis to name a few.

By the age of 37, she married a fellow teacher. They were blessed with a baby only to be taken in death as an infant. Some say that this was what inspired her to write the following song:

Safe in the Arms of Jesus

Safe in the arms of Jesus,
Safe on His gentle breast;
There by His love o'ershaded,
Sweetly my soul shall rest.
Hark! 'Tis the voice of angels
Borne in a song to me,
Over the fields of glory,
Over the jasper sea.

Refrain

Safe in the arms of Jesus,
Safe on His gentle breast;
There by His love o'ershaded,
Sweetly my soul shall rest.

Safe in the arms of Jesus,
Safe from corroding care,
Safe from the world's temptations;
Sin cannot harm me there.
Free from the blight of sorrow,
Free from my doubts and fears;
Only a few more trials,
Only a few more tears!

Jesus, my heart's dear Refuge,
Jesus has died for me;
Firm on the Rock of Ages
Ever my trust shall be.
Here let me wait with patience,
Wait till the night is o'er;
Wait till I see the morning
Break on the golden shore.

This song would be one among the thousands of hymns that Fanny would write in her lifetime. Over 8,000 have been documented.

Some of her greatest songs were: "Blessed Assurance," "To God Be the Glory," "Saved by Grace" and "Near the Cross" to name a few. She allowed God to use her and did not give in to self-pity because of her blindness. It was because of her blindness that she was inspired to write and tell of God's goodness. Fanny Crosby will always be an inspiration to me for the way she handled adversity. Her faith was strong, and she enjoyed sharing it with others. It was her calling. Like Fanny, every Christian has a mission to share the love and hope of Jesus Christ!

Make a choice today to live like you "believe," and you can bounce back with the blessed assurance that Jesus is with you.

Blessed Assurance
by Fanny Crosby

Blessed assurance, Jesus is mine!
Oh, what a foretaste of glory divine!
Heir of salvation, purchase of God,
Born of His Spirit, washed in His blood.

Refrain
This is my story, this is my song,
Praising my Savior all the day long;
This is my story, this is my song,
Praising my Savior all the day long.

Perfect submission, perfect delight,
Visions of rapture now burst on my sight;
Angels descending, bring from above
Echoes of mercy, whispers of love.

Perfect submission, all is at rest,
I in my Savior am happy and blest,
Watching and waiting, looking above,
Filled with His goodness, lost in His love.

I was reading one of Randy Alcorn's books and found this about a woman named Ann Stump. She made a statement that speaks to my heart. This is what she said after her 18-month-old son's death:

> I learned what it was like not to be able to do something on my own. I couldn't get up in the morning without the Lord's help. He can bear the weight of our pain and give us strength and life when we are at our weakest.

God's Sovereignty in Suffering

Maybe Fanny Crosby's secret to resilience was the fact that she recognized God's sovereignty in suffering. She must have come to the conclusion early on in her life that God was ultimately in control of all things.

Unfortunately, it has taken me many years to finally come to that conclusion. I'm sure I could have saved myself and my family a lot of unnecessary grief and pain. However, it's a very difficult place to get to. It's a mindset that we have to grasp and not let go of, for if we do, we will miss out on the many blessings that our Heavenly Father has in store for us.

Once we can finally rest in the sovereignty of an Almighty God, our hearts can be receptive to His plans that He has for us. Instead of chasing our dreams and being disheartened and disillusioned when they don't come to pass, we can rest in the fact that He does all things well.

God's Word tells us that He knows all things in the past, present, and what is to come in the future (Romans 11:33). God can do anything, and there is nothing too difficult for Him (Jeremiah 32:17). Satan even has to ask God's permission before he can act (Psalm 103:19).

I have heard my grandmother say to me many times that there is nothing that happens to a child of God that doesn't pass through the hands of our loving Father first. She would say to me, "God is sovereign. God is just."

I have asked God many times over why He didn't choose to heal Jacob. He could have done so by touching him with His infinite power. God is able to heal, but sometimes He chooses not to react in the way that we want Him to. He has a reason. He has a purpose that our minds cannot comprehend.

If you are struggling with these questions, you can find peace and contentment on your journey when you get to the point that you can say and believe wholeheartedly that, "God is in control."

We were made for His glory, and as we look at the lives of many heroes of the faith, we can see that their lives and their pain were not in vain. We can pattern our lives after those who have persevered in the face of death, persecution, and pain.

If we live our lives never yielding to the fact that we were made to bring Him glory, then we are defeating our purpose to live. Once we surrender to the reason we were put here on this earth, we can live with real purpose and be content in serving Jesus. We can leave our troubles behind and learn from them. We can live with a determination to let our light shine so that others around us will want what we have. We can experience true joy for the journey!

There are times when God seems distant, and we can't seem to hear His voice. It's usually because we have pushed Him away. We are good at building up walls of bitterness towards Him when we can't comprehend His ways. I have done that myself many times. It has been over ten years now since Jacob's birth and death, and fortunately, I am finally surrendering to God's sovereignty.

The following was a journal writing of mine from July 2014, which became lyrics to a song:

God Is
Copyright 2014

When God is silent and you cannot hear His voice
When Hope is buried 'neath the rubble of your
brokenness
When Joy somehow seems so unattainable
There's a comfort just to know

Refrain

God is sovereign. God is just.
When He is silent we must trust;
He is working all things for our good.
God is able. God is waiting.
To give you hope and He is saying
Come to all those who are heavy laden
God is.

When love seems lost and nothing seems to satisfy
When all your dreams have failed, your heart's
breaking inside
When everything around you is enough to ask God why
Stand still and realize
(Refrain)

Chapter 19

The Refiner's Fire

"Satan wishes to destroy our faith through suffering, God desires to refine it."
Randy Acorn

It was a cold winter's morning on Feb. 20, 2010, that would prove to be a life changing event for our small family of three. A thin layer of frost lay on the ground outside of our thirty-year-old cabin nestled in the mountains of Tennessee. We had purchased our home a few years before when we moved from Florida. We loved living in Tennessee, and we were enjoying life in the mountains! Yes, life was grand.

Our stone fireplace had been lit the night before, which made our Friday evening at home all the more cozy. We decided to spend the evening at home watching our DVD's of *Little House on the Prairie*. I had managed to do some cleaning as well, dusting and vacuuming our log walls and ceilings. The dust and cobwebs were hard to see, and I had been slack concerning that particular chore for a while. By the time I had finished, I felt like I had really accomplished something. My house was officially "clean," or at least, as clean as I could get a log cabin without getting splinters in my hands! We finally went to bed that night around midnight.

All was quiet on our hill in the wee hours of that cold Saturday morning. We were snug in our bed, which was layered with quilts to keep us nice and warm. Isaac was in his usual spot, between us!

Surprisingly, Anthony awoke very early. I expected him to sleep a little longer than usual because of his stressful week and with our going to bed so late the night before. He went downstairs to his office around 7:45 A.M. As he was sitting there, barely awake, he heard a loud noise that sounded like someone shooting a gun.

We live in the country, so that was not unusual. Eventually, he started smelling something like an electrical fire. He got up, followed the smell, and found to his amazement that the entire front side of our cabin was on fire!

Isaac and I were still upstairs sleeping when I heard Anthony's voice filled with fear, yelling to the top of his lungs, "Cindy, GO GET ISAAC!" As I started down the stairs to see what was happening, I found our living room going up in flames! Anthony had opened the front door where we discovered the fire had started. Our two propane tanks had exploded on our front porch.

When Anthony opened the door and attempted to put the fire out, the pressure knocked him backwards. At that point, it was too late! The flames were licking across the ceiling and traveling rapidly throughout the entire house. I ran back upstairs and grabbed Isaac, and the three of us ran for our lives, bringing the black smoke out with us.

As we exited the back door of our Tennessee cabin, we realized how blessed we were to have made it out alive. Isaac was reaching towards the back of the house crying for his toys. I immediately told him that we would get more toys and that we were going to be okay.

Anthony had managed to grab his cell phone and the keys to his car. He called 911, and I rushed to the neighbor's house screaming all the way. They immediately took Isaac inside and began entertaining him with Mario Cart video games to get his mind off of the tragedy. I later found out that they also cooked him a country breakfast which he still talks about to this day. Thankfully, that's the memory in his little mind that overshadows the tragedy of our fire. Their house proved to be his safe haven and a place of refuge that he will never forget. I am so grateful for that.

I ran back over to our burning house and stood beside my husband. He put his arm around me and said, "Cindy, it's gone ... everything is gone. I can't believe this is happening." We were in shock. It really WAS hard to believe.

Cabin on fire
This picture was taken ten minutes afer we got out.
February 20, 2010

On a funny note, while we were waiting for the fire department to arrive, which seemed like an eternity, Anthony looked at me and said, "What am I gonna do? I am in my underwear, and the fire department is coming." I immediately thought about the scarecrow in our barn that I had never undressed from fall. It had Anthony's old jeans on it, so it was perfect. He grabbed the frozen jeans off the scarecrow and put them on. By that time, our neighbor had come over with one of his jackets and handed it to him. Now, my husband is 6'3", and our neighbor is quite a bit smaller in stature. You can imagine what a funny sight that was. The arms of the jacket were about 2 inches too short, and it barely covered his stomach! At least he had something to keep him warm! This was proof that God provides!

The first person on the scene was one of our church deacons. He arrived before the fire department. I remember standing in the backyard looking at our dining room window with flames shooting out. I told him that my journals were on my table, and I really needed them for my book. Of course, there was no way of getting them out at that point.

All of my journals dated 1999-2010 were lying on this dining room table where I was using them to write this book.

All of my journals, along with my computer, my Bible, and my notes were spread across the dining room table. That was my "work- space." The Lord had placed a burden in my heart to share my faith journey with others to tell how He had brought me through a difficult part of my life and how He had helped me to continue to live in victory by calling me to write this book that you are now reading.

I knew that my journals were a very important part in the process. These were very close to my heart and were among the "things" in our cabin that I considered to be "irreplaceable."

I began journaling in 1999 when my sister-in-law encouraged me to express my feelings on paper as I dealt with my infertility. I never dreamed that the journals would be something that the Lord would use in this book. They were filled with all the times that the Lord whispered words of comfort and peace to my heart, not only through my years of barrenness, but through the news of becoming a mother for the first time, the death of our precious baby boy, and the miraculous way that Isaac came into our lives.

These journals have been a stimulus to my faith journey and have held precious moments spent with the Master. They held the words of the songs that God would give to me during and after my night season.

Within a short time after the fire department arrived, our church family began filtering in one by one, bringing us bags of clothing and toys for Isaac. After the fire was out and all that was left were ashes and an unforgettable smoldering smoke smell that filled our nostrils, our pastor gathered everyone in a large circle in our backyard and led us in a time of prayer.

My husband, being the strong man of faith that he was and still is, said, "This fire is just another bump in the road and we will make it. We are grateful to be alive and have each other. Things can be replaced, but people can't. My grandfather has always said that you never see a U-Haul behind a hearse. We came into this world with nothing and will take nothing with us when we leave it."

He continued to encourage us that day reminding us that the Lord has always taken care of us and provided all of our needs. Once again, his faith was strong even through the fire!

Those standing around us in that beautiful circle of love reached out to us in so many ways. A couple from our church allowed us to stay in an apartment that was next to their house until our house was rebuilt. They took us in as though we were family. As a matter of fact, they took us home with them that evening and gave us their master suite to sleep in. Although I didn't do much sleeping that night, it was a very comfortable bed. We lacked for nothing and had all the comforts of "home," and most importantly, we had each other. There we were the three of us in a king-size bed with Isaac in his usual spot, in the middle!

I lay there that night staring into the darkness, wide awake. I couldn't fathom what had actually taken place. However, I knew in my heart that everything would be okay and that we would somehow start over and life would go on. Besides, this was nothing compared to the death of Jacob.

The next morning, we got up, got ready for church, and went to teach our Sunday school class of five year olds. We sang in the choir, not in our own strength, but only through the power and strength that God alone can give. Once again, we were experiencing God's sustaining grace. The Lord was our provider.

Our family had arrived from Florida earlier that morning and brought us clothes. After church that day, Carl & Linda, who had taken us in, prepared a huge meal of chicken and dumplings with all the fixing to go with it. This was what I call comfort food! Once again, the Lord provided!

As I stood in their kitchen that day after lunch, I remember getting teary eyed when I thought about my journals. I just couldn't understand why God would allow something so special and so important to the completion of my book to be destroyed.

We decided to stay home from church that evening to sort through some of the rubble from the fire. Some of our friends from church had set some things to the side that they thought could be salvaged. Even though everything was black and charred, we began looking through it that Sunday evening. Everything had that same horrible smell; a smell that has forever changed the way we think about fire when we see it or smell it.

It was beginning to get dark when my husband said, "Cindy, you might want to take a look at what I've found." What he showed me thrilled my heart. It was all of my journals!

They were almost unrecognizable from the outside, but when I opened them carefully, I could read each of the pages! They were singed around the edges and wet from the fire hoses. That evening, Linda and I tore out each page, numbered them, and laid them out to dry.

This experience has reminded me once again that God is in control and that He orders our steps and goes before us. If our deacon

Pages from my journals

had not arrived at the scene of the fire when he did and had not heard me mention my journals, they would have been thrown away that day. As a matter of fact, he later told me that someone was going to throw them away, but he told them to save them for me just in case something could be done with them.

That was the first of many other sentimental items that the Lord preserved for us from the fire. Another very special "something" that could not be replaced was my gold heart locket. It had Jacob's picture on one side and Isaac's on the other. Isaac had opened it in the past and pointed to the pictures in it. He pointed to Jacob's picture, looking toward the sky and said, "Jacob is in Heaven." I was able to use that locket to share with Isaac that if we have Jesus in our heart, we can go to Heaven where Jacob is one day. That has given him a longing to go to Heaven even as a young child and is what prompted him to want to be saved at the early age of four.

Our pastor was the one that found my locket the day of the fire. It was still hanging on the side of my dresser where I had left it the night before. The chain was ruined, but the gold locket was still intact. It was blackened, but had not melted.

When I opened the locket that day, I found both pictures unsinged and perfectly in place. Later, I took it to a jeweler, along with my wedding rings and other gold items. I told him how special the locket was to me, and he immediately began working on it. A few minutes passed, and he brought it to me. Amazingly, it was even more beautiful than ever. It was bright and shiny once again. There was still a dent in the middle of the heart from

Isaac's teeth mark, and that made it even more precious to me. When I had held him on my hip, he'd play with that locket and sometimes bite down on it. That was something I could have never replaced!

When I think of all of the events that took place during and after our house fire, I can't help but think about the refiner's fire and how God uses the fiery trials of life to mold us into what He wants us to be. It's through the fire that the imperfections of our hearts are melted away until He can see His reflection.

My sister-in-law shared a wonderful women's devotion with me that pertains to this subject and I would love to share it with you in order to expound on the thought of the refiner's fire. The following is the devotion and a post from a reader:

"He shall sit as a refiner and purifier of silver..."

This verse puzzled the women and they wondered what this statement meant about the character and nature of God. One of the women offered to find out about the process of refining silver and get back to the group at their next Bible study.

That week this woman called up a silversmith and made an appointment to watch him at work. She didn't mention anything about the reason for the interest in silver beyond her curiosity about the process of refining silver. As she watched the silversmith, he held a piece of silver over the fire and let it heat up. He explained that in refining silver, one needed to hold the silver in the middle of the fire where the flames were hottest so as to burn away all the impurities.

The woman thought about God holding us in such a hot spot. Then she thought again about the verse, *"He shall sit as a refiner and purifier of silver."* She asked the silversmith if it was true that he had to sit there in front of the fire the whole time the silver was being refined. The man answered yes. He not only had to sit there holding the silver, but he had to keep his eyes on the silver the entire time it was in the fire. For if the silver was left even a moment too long in the flames, it would be destroyed.

The woman was silent for a moment. Then she asked the silversmith, "How do you know when the silver is fully refined?" He smiled at her and answered, "Oh that's the easy part, when I see my image reflected in it."

Author Unknown

Passed out at the: Valley Church of Christ Ladies Retreat 2005 Wasilla, Alaska –Posted by Mrs. M at 9:31 A.M.

Anonymous said:

As the familiar story passed before my eyes it warmed my heart but it was in the part that I could not recall (found herein) upon which dawn broke & wherein the true power lies: He is waiting and watching for His reflection to appear. This is all I've ever wanted to know: will I be made over into His image? Will this make me like Jesus? If I can endure this and get that it will all be worthwhile. I don't need to be afraid for this I know and am reminded of: His eye is on the sparrow and He's watching over me … sitting as a refiner and a purifier of silver … and when He has tried me, I shall come forth as gold:) ... and as for my Enemy this much I also know: he who touches me touches the apple of His eye. I am being made over into HIS image, and I need not fear the flames; I shall come forth as gold. Amen! Thank you, Jesus!

Though at times the fire gets hot on our faith journey, the Lord will not allow us to be destroyed.

During the refining process, the heat of the furnace is critical, if too severe then the silver or gold will be vaporized and lost, if too cold then some of the lead will remain and the metal will not be pure. The smith watches the temperature very closely to make sure that it stays exactly right. In other words, the severity of our trials is extremely important to God, for He wants us to be pure and never to be lost. In 1 Cor 10:13, our God, who cannot lie, promises that He will not tempt or test us beyond what we are able to cope with (*God the Refiner* by Russell Barnett).

I Pet 5:10

And after you have suffered for a little while, the God of all grace, who called you to His eternal glory in Christ, will Himself perfect, confirm, strengthen and establish you."

Ultimately, it is God's plan for us to be refined God requires us to be like precious, pure silver, to have a pure heart free of all dross and impurities.

As the silver or gold nears the final stage of refining it experiences an action known as "brightening." This happens when the remainder of the impurities are consumed. The now pure molten metal suddenly emits a bright flash of light and immediately solidifies. I eagerly look forward to the time when God sees this happen to His people.

Russell Barnett

Lord, may we shine bright with the light of your love, and as the refiner of silver and gold, may you refine us until your reflection is what the world sees.

From the outside looking in ... looks can be deceiving on the surface!

We might look good on the outside and do a pretty good job of acting like we've got it all together. We put on our Sunday best, painting on our pretty smiles, even when we feel like we are ready to give up on life. I have done that many times. We are good at faking kindness when it's not really coming from our hearts. This is what I call "lip service," and I am guilty of this as well.

Often we are holding grudges, becoming bitter, and eventually allowing walls to be built up between us, our loved ones, and most importantly, the Lord.

None of these things go unnoticed by God. Just as a father and mother nurtures, corrects, and teaches their children in the way that they should go, our Heavenly Father corrects us when necessary. Sometimes God uses fire to teach and correct us. In doing so, He refines and purifies us.

Our cabin may have looked beautiful on the surface. If you would have peeked in the windows, you would have seen a warm and cozy home that seemed very inviting to most visitors. In reality, it was the draftiest house

I'd ever lived in! The wind blew right through those thirty-year-old windows. On a cold winter's night, we were chilled to the bone unless we sat next to the fireplace.

Everything on the surface might have looked nice and clean. However, the crevices in the log walls held dust and cobwebs that couldn't even be seen unless light was cast on them from a certain angle.

The structure of our cabin "looked" to be strong and durable, but no one could see that is was "rotten" and infested with carpenter bees that had destroyed the logs. As the fire department began climbing up the back wall the day of the fire, pieces of it began to fall to the ground.

There have been times in my life when I didn't realize the "dross" or the "rotten" places in my heart. My mind was filled with cobwebs that had accumulated over time because I had neglected my "spiritual" cleaning that takes place when I spend time in prayer and Bible study.

In order to know how dirty the "windows" of my heart are, I ask myself important questions at times. These are reflected in the following journal writing:

Windows of my heart ... Journal from 9/3/12

As He's looking through the windows of my heart, what does He see? What will He find in me? Will He find I'm being all that I should be? Am I pleasing in His sight when He shines His light into the places no one else can see?

Do I do and say the things He'd have me say, or am I getting in His way?

Have I surrendered my all to Him each and every day?

When I ask myself these questions, it helps me strive to be a better Christian and makes me want to do more for Him!

When others are looking from the outside in, may they not be deceived ... things might not quite be as they seem. Lord, help me examine myself from the inside out, so what you and others find is pleasing to you.

Make sure your windows of your heart are clean from the inside out!

Matthew Henry's Concise Commentary

He shall sit as a refiner. Christ, by His gospel, shall purify and reform His church, and by His Spirit working with it, shall regenerate and cleanse souls. He will take away the dross found in them. He will separate their corruptions, which render their faculties worthless and useless. The believer needs not fear the fiery trial of afflictions and temptations, by which the Savior refines His gold. He will take care it is not more intense or longer than is needful for his good. ... Because we have to do with a God that changes not; therefore, it is that we are not consumed, because His compassions fail not.

A Living Hope

Matthew Henry's Concise Commentary

Hope, in the world's phrase, refers only to an uncertain good, for all worldly hopes are tottering, built upon sand, and the worldling's hopes of

Heaven are blind and groundless conjectures. But the hope of the sons of the living God is a living hope; not only as to its object, but as to its effect also. It enlivens and comforts in all distresses, enables to meet and get over all difficulties. Mercy is the spring of all this; yea, great mercy and manifold mercy. And this well-grounded hope of salvation is an active and living principle of obedience in the soul of the believer.

The matter of a Christian's joy is the remembrance of the happiness laid up for him. It is incorruptible. It is an estate that cannot be spent. Also undefiled, this signifies its purity and perfection. And it fadeth not; is not sometimes more or less pleasant, but ever the same, still like itself.

All possessions here are stained with defects and failings; still something is wanting: fair houses have sad cares flying about the gilded and ceiled roofs; soft beds and full tables are often with sick bodies and uneasy stomachs. All possessions are stained with sin, either in getting or in using them. How ready we are to turn the things we possess into occasions and instruments of sin, and to think there is no liberty or delight in their use, without abusing them!

Worldly possessions are uncertain and soon pass away, like the flowers and plants of the field. That must be of the greatest worth, which is laid up in the highest and best place, in Heaven. Happy are those whose hearts the Holy Spirit sets on this inheritance. God not only gives His people grace, but preserves them unto glory. Every believer has always something wherein he may greatly rejoice; it should show itself in the countenance and conduct.

The Lord does not willingly afflict, yet His wise love often appoints sharp trials to show His people their hearts, and to do them good at the latter end. Gold does not increase by trial in the fire; it becomes less; but faith is made firm, and multiplied by troubles and afflictions. Gold must perish at last, and can only purchase perishing things, while the trial of faith will be found to praise, and honor, and glory. Let this reconcile us to present afflictions.

Seek then to believe Christ's excellence in himself, and His love to us; this will kindle such a fire in the heart as will make it rise up in a sacrifice of love to Him. And the glory of God and our own happiness are so united, that if we sincerely seek the one now, we shall attain the other when the soul shall no more be subject to evil.

Before the fiery trial of losing Jacob, I was a person that struggled to have my own way and neglected the fact that God should be in control of my life. I had a heart that might have looked fine on the surface, but from the inside out it was not a pretty picture. The windows of my heart were filled with things that were not pleasing to the Lord.

I now know from experience that God's Word never fails, and I am thankful for the "fire" that He allowed me to walk thru in order for Him to change me into His likeness. I have not "arrived" by any means, but I can say now that I have a clearer picture of what my purpose is in life and that it is to serve and love the Lord with all my heart, my mind, and soul while spreading His message of hope! My perspective and purpose in life have changed drastically. It's no longer about "ME."

From the very day that our house and contents were destroyed by the fire, my husband and I have said, it really was just another bump in the road. I truly believe that the death of Jacob brought things into perspective for me. It made me realize what is truly important in life, and it's not the material things that this world can offer. I have learned that only Jesus Christ can satisfy our hearts and fill us with an expected hope of glory that yet awaits His children in Heaven.

The fiery trial that I walked through in 2004 when Jacob left this earth, has changed me forever. It has changed the way I think, the way I live, and has made me even more determined to make my life and his life count for Christ! I have finally said "Yes" to the Lord and His perfect will for my life. I can see now that it took the "fire" to bring me to that place of total surrender. Yes, Total Surrender = Total Contentment and Joy!

If you are walking through the fire or just came out of one, remember, your hope lies in Jesus Christ. You will be stronger as a result of your trial as you allow God to mold you into His image.

I encourage you today, yield to the potter. Yield to the refiner and you will come forth as gold,' and in due time you will reap a harvest of bountiful blessings.

God uses suffering as a way to bring us to total reliance on Him realizing we can do nothing on our own.
Randy Alcorn

Scriptures

Psalm 66:10

For you, O God, have proved us: you have tried us, as silver is tried.

Proverbs 17:3

The fining pot is for silver, and the furnace for gold: but the LORD trieth the hearts.

Proverbs 25:4

Take away the dross from the silver, and there shall come forth a vessel for the refiner.

1 Peter 5:10 English Standard Version (ESV)

And after you have suffered a little while, the God of all grace, who has called you to His eternal glory in Christ, will himself restore, confirm, strengthen, and establish you.

Job 23:10 ESV

But he knows the way that I take; when he has tried me, I shall come out as gold.

1 Peter 1:6-7 ESV

In this you rejoice, though now for a little while, if necessary, you have been grieved by various trials, that the trial of your faith, being much more precious than gold that perishes though tested by fire, may be found to result in praise and glory and honor at the revelation of Jesus Christ.

James 1:3

Because you know that the testing of your faith produces perseverance.

Chapter 20

Broken Dreams

We all have our own agenda filled with the dreams we'd like to attain in life. I'm not talking about dreaming of a "White Christmas." I'm talking about our hearts' deepest desires for our lives. They are important to us. We dream big and there is nothing wrong with that. However, we need to be careful and include God in our dreams. We need to consult Him and pray for His perfect will to be accomplished in our lives making sure that our desires line up with His Word.

Jeremiah 29:11 says, *"For I know the plans I have for you sayeth the Lord, not of evil but of good, to give you a future and a hope."*

God has His own agenda, and most of the time it's not the story that we have written for our faith journey. We go our own way never thinking twice about what He might have had planned for us, and most of the time we get ahead of Him and make a mess of things. That's why God has to get our attention and take us on some detours, so we can be used best by Him for His glory.

> *"Some saints are awakened by a tap on the shoulder while others need a two-by-four to the head."*
> Max Lucado (*The Great House of God*)

Apparently, I was one of the ones that needed the two-by-four!

Most everyone has had dreams that have not been attained. We could easily roll around in self-pity, but that won't do anything but hurt us. We must not dwell on the past. Sometimes, I start feeling sorry for myself if I allow my thoughts to go in a certain direction. If I allow myself to walk down a path from the past and begin to relive the pain, I suffer for it. I have slowly begun to realize that God is really good at taking our broken dreams and putting the pieces back together the way He sees fit. The following journal explains:

12/9/13 Journal ... Broken Dreams—Buried Treasures

O.K., I cried my eyes out last night. Something came over me, and I'm sure that "something" was Satan trying to oppress me. He knows what buttons to push. Even though it's been nine years since Jacob went to be with Jesus, I still struggle at times; however, I don't linger in that frame of mind for very long.

I started thinking of the dreams I have buried and that I continue to bury. It's those dreams that I've had since I was a child and still have, to this day at 44 years old. I had to bury my first dream in 2004 when Jacob went to be with Jesus. I had to let him go. The Lord has helped me handle that disappointment, but last night I was thinking of all the dreams that have not been fulfilled in my life. I had sure hoped by now after 25 years of marriage, that the Lord would have blessed us with another child. And that has not happened, and I'm getting too old. Myra, my mother-in-love, told me to change my dreams. She was blunt, but I needed that. It's time for me to allow God to change my dreams!

Yes, I am feeling sorry for myself and having a pity party. I don't normally attend these types of parties, and don't intend to in the future. However, sometimes I feel like I just have to cry. I know it's okay to cry as long as I don't stay in that frame of mind and do not cry as if there is no hope.

I told Anthony that I needed a firm talking to and for him to set me straight, and of course, he did. Thank the Lord for a godly husband that can put things into perspective when my faith has gotten off track. I'm well on my way again to travel this faith journey! He reminded me that this life is temporary and that we shouldn't lay up our treasures here on earth. We are here to accomplish the Father's will and not ours. Again, I needed to be reminded that Heaven is waiting and that it is what really matters most because one day soon we will be there forever!

As you can see, even though it has been many years since Jacob's death, Satan still lurks and sneaks around trying to devour me. I made a choice a long time ago that when he tries to block my view of the battles that I have already won, I will stand and claim the victory, in Jesus name, and I will overcome!

The Lord immediately turned my brief pity party into a testimony of praise and victory for His sake! That pity party inspired me to right this chapter and a song. That's what I call giving the devil a black eye! Wham!!!

Dreaming Joseph …

When I think about dreamers, I can't help but refer to one of the greatest heroes of the Bible, Joseph. Keep in mind as we look at his life that the Lord was with Joseph as he faced every obstacle and many disappointments. God gave Joseph dreams, and they came to pass. However, if Joseph were here today, I'm sure that he would say that those dreams weren't the ones he had for himself. God had other plans that were far different from his; however, it would be worth it for Christ's sake in the end.

JOSEPH

✦ His gift: Interpreting dreams

✦ His sorrow: He was betrayed by his family. His brothers were jealous of him and wanted him dead.

✦ His treasure: A very special gift given to him by his father was a coat of many colors. It was taken from him by his brothers when they threw him in a pit and left him there to die.

✦ More sorrow: He was thrown in jail after being sold as a slave.

✦ His strength: After setbacks, he learned humility, wisdom and forgiveness.

Joseph experienced many hardships, but continued to trust in God and because of his obedience, God used him for His glory!

Joseph's life is a prime example of what can happen when a person surrenders to GOD! Obedience is the key!

What will it take for us to become obedient and surrender our wants and desires to Christ? Will it take hardship? Will it take death? Oh, if we could just consecrate ourselves in total submission and total trust to the Master, we would save ourselves a lot of pain and a lot of time on our faith journey.

Some of us like Joseph have been betrayed by family, maybe even through divorce. Some of us might have had to bury treasures and have faced the death of someone very dear to us. Many have been like Joseph and been thrown into a pit, maybe even jail, and left for dead. They have felt like hope has been buried forever.

Take heart my friend! Just as the Lord was with Joseph, the Lord is with us! He is on our side and He is for us! He gets the last word and His Word tells us that we are more than conquerors through Christ Jesus!

Lord, help us to live each day by faith, in total consecration to you ready to accept the call to serve with a willing heart. Help us to give our dreams to you so that you can fulfill your purpose in our lives.

Broken Dreams & Buried Treasures
Lyrics by Cindy Johnson
(copyright 2014)

I've had to bury treasures
That were so dear to me
My heart has been broken
Sometimes I could hardly see

But hope came knocking at my door
And my faith turned into sight
He gave healing for my brokenness
Turned my darkness into light!

Refrain

Broken dreamed & buried treasures
Let Jesus put the pieces back together
What you long to hold so close within your arms
Is being held by the Father for a little while
So give Jesus all your broken dreams &
buried treasures.

A life full of disappointments
Of dreams that were unachieved
You've been bound by chains of bitterness
Traveling a road of misery
But don't lose sight of your tomorrows
Jesus has a perfect plan
And every dream that you've ever dreamed
He's holding in His hands!

I am still seeing glimpses of God's glory in my life as
I continue to yield my heart to Him. God has brought me
through things I thought I'd never survive. I'm still
learning to trust along the way, and as I've taken each
step of faith, He has given me the grace. I take comfort in
knowing that He's holding some of my dreams in Heaven
for me until I get there.

I am thankful that He far surpassed my wildest
dreams with the blessing of Isaac. Isaac has certainly

lived up to the meaning of his name by bringing many smiles to my face at some of my weakest moments. God has used him to encourage me many times along the way.

Journal writing 3/12/11

"I love you, Mom." That's what Isaac kept telling me tonight after church. He looked up at me with those big brown eyes and told me he loved me several times. After about the fourth time, I studied his face to see if there was an ulterior motive. I could tell by the look in his eyes and his expression that he was telling me "just because." Those words sounded like music to my ears and reminded me what a miracle he was in my life.

Now isn't that just like God to bring healing to my "sinking" heart today? I had struggled this past week with thoughts of Jacob and his death. The Lord used three little words from my miracle baby as a balm for my heart. (Psalms 147 says, *"He heals the broken hearted and binds up their wounds."* When my old wounds are opened, He brings healing and comfort in my time of need. Isaac says, "Mommy, Jesus heals all our 'boo-boos,'" and he is right.

There's a settled peace within my heart today as I reflect on God's faithfulness and the blessings He continues to bestow upon me and my family. And to think, God loves me, just because. That's pretty amazing. The One, who knows me best, loves me best.

God continues to bless me with so many other priceless treasures. He's given me inspiration to pen these words. I NEVER dreamed that I would be writing songs or writing a book. I never dreamed that I would be singing and sharing my testimony of victory in churches and ladies' events.

Thankfully, God does not always call the qualified, but qualifies the called. Like Joseph, His dream for us is bigger than we are.

Buried Treasures ...

What treasure have you had to bury? What hurt or disappointments are you still holding onto and just can't seem to let go? It's a very difficult task and took me awhile to let Jacob go. However, my heart is finally at peace because I know where he is and that I will hold him again one day. The memories of Jacob are ones when I was pregnant with him and the few days that he was alive in the NICU. I choose not to dwell on the pain and hurt. I choose daily to dwell on where God has brought me from and how He will use Jacob's life and death for His glory.

Miraculously there were a few keepsakes of Jacob's that made it through our house fire. I had a special box that I used for his "things" from the hospital: his blanket, a card with his name on it, a pair of overalls with his name embroidered on them, pictures from my pregnancy and of him, as well as my pregnancy journal. I used to keep this special box of "keepsakes" beside my bed.

A few weeks before the fire, I moved it to our spare bedroom. Almost everything in our bedroom was totally destroyed. However, Jacob's box along with a few other irreplaceable items that were in the spare bedroom were miraculously saved. God preserved the items in that box.

All I had to do was wash them and purchase something else to put his things in.

Keep this comforting thought in mind. God is holding your "treasure" in Heaven. Heaven's holding something special that you, too, will hold one day.

Journal (4/26/12)

Isaac helped me place Jacob's things into a new keepsake box. As he was looking through everything with me, he was humming and singing the tune, "'Tis, So Sweet to Trust In Jesus." He looked up at me with those big brown eyes making sure I was "O.K." I assured him that I was just fine.

As we continued to sort thru the priceless treasures, we came across the picture of Jacob that the hospital had taken after he passed away. Needless to say, I was never able to look at it very much. I had glanced at it a few times, but that was all. It was a pitiful and sad sight. Isaac looked up at me and said, "Remember Mommy, God had a plan." As I flipped to the next picture, it was a picture of Isaac with a huge smile. I replied, "Yes, God did have a plan and it was YOU!"

Sometimes He may change the course of our journey and may even change our dreams. But, whatever road we may travel, we can rest assured He'll lead, through every mountain, every valley, and sometimes His hand is unseen. That's where faith steps in, and we can trust His plan will far exceed anything we ever hoped for, every dream we've ever dreamed.

Chapter 21

When God Says, "Wait"

"Fill your arms with hope until He fills them with reality."
Edna Shevock

Before Jacob and Isaac came along, I worked in the banking industry. I remember many days, sitting behind my desk, wondering when God would answer my prayer and give me the desires of my heart. I was miserable and was tired of waiting on God. However, in retrospect, this part of my journey has proven to be one of the highlights for me because I now see that God had an eternal purpose in mind. I have found that when God says, "wait," it is for Heaven's sake, for HIS sake and for the sake of others around me.

My office was located in the middle of a large retirement facility that overlooked a beautiful golf course. My clientele were all retirees. Many opened up to me at times and shared the difficulties that they were going through. I used every opportunity that I could to point them to Christ.

One day, the Lord sent a very special lady into my life for a very special reason. Her name was Edna. I'd never met anyone quite like her. She was one of my customers and very quickly became part of my "mission" while I was in the "waiting" mode on my journey. She was blunt, funny, witty, extremely intelligent, and what I'd call a little "crazy" at times. I truly loved her! As soon as I met her, my heart broke for her. She had bone cancer and had lost all of her hair from the chemo and radiation treatments; nevertheless, she rejected pity from anyone! She must have seen the pain and compassion in my eyes, the day I met her, and bluntly said, "Hey, don't feel sorry for me, kid."

Edna had a wig for every day of the week. She wore what she called her Tina Turner wig, a Marilyn Monroe wig, a Lucy wig and a Cher wig! She even took her wig off while sitting in my office to show everyone her bald head! You never knew what Edna would do or say next.

She was a woman of many words, and some of those words were not in my vocabulary. She could have made a sailor blush. I asked her very nicely one day if she would please refrain from using that type of language, and her reply was, "Honey, it's just words." She was a retired high-school teacher and told me that she had to have a "come-back" for her students. Most of them came from challenging backgrounds, and it would be reflected in their attitude towards her.

Edna and I came from two totally different backgrounds and were as opposite as the day is long; however, God gave me favor with her. She had not been brought up in a Christian home and had never accepted the Lord as her Savior. The only experience she had in church was when she, as a child, occasionally attended a Baptist church in her neighborhood.

The longer I worked in that community, the more I realized that there were many other hurting people that needed the Lord. I finally realized that I was on a "mission field" in my own town. Eventually, the Lord gave my husband's grandfather a burden to start a church in that community. He had been in the ministry for over 60 years and still had a heart for souls. He passed away in 2013, and I am proud to say that the church is still thriving, and many souls have been saved as a result of his obedience to the call.

I invited Edna to our community church many times. After all, it was convenient. She could even drive her golf cart to get there. It was located in the ballroom in the clubhouse. Sadly, Edna never came. She always slept late into the morning hours.

My heart was burdened for her soul as well as for her health condition. I wanted so badly to fix her problems. I knew that I couldn't do that, but I knew Someone who could. I began to pray for Edna. There were many nights when I would lie awake in bed, begging God to somehow save her. It really looked impossible. She seemed hardened by the pain and understandably so. I wondered how God was ever going to get through to her. I knew it would take a miracle.

I continued to pray and cry out to God on Edna's behalf. In the meantime, I decided I would plan a special ladies' luncheon for the community. The theme was, "Joy for the Journey." I hired a caterer and a special speaker. It was a way for me to reach out to many women that didn't know the Lord. I invited Edna to come. She agreed and came walking in, in rare form, flaunting her Tina Turner Wig, bright red lipstick, and a black sequin blouse! As you can imagine, the other ladies kept their distance not knowing how to take her.

The special speaker that day was someone I had admired for years. She spoke with such compassion that I was sure it would soften Edna's hardened heart towards accepting Christ. After she shared her closing thoughts that day, Edna stood up, took off her wig, and began to weep. She told everyone about her struggle with cancer. I was shocked, as well as the other 100 ladies in attendance that day.

Edna proceeded to tell the group of women how God had been dealing with her heart – telling them about a gospel concert that I had invited her to a few months before. She told them of the hope that shined through the message in each song that she heard that night. She had been so moved by the singing that she turned to me with eyeliner running down her cheeks and said, "I hope you are happy now." I knew then that the Holy Spirit was at work! She purchased every CD on the product table after the concert. She had never been to an event like that before.

As Edna continued to tell her story, I saw several ladies wiping tears from their eyes. She had touched the lives of the people there that day. I could plainly see that God was not finished with her yet.

A few years later, Jacob came along and then Isaac arrived. I was officially a stay-at-home mom. Two years passed, and my husband's company offered him a position in Tennessee. We prayed about it and both agreed that it was the Lord's will for our family. I knew before I left town that I had to see Edna one more time. I had to witness to her once more and try to lead her to Christ. It had been a total of seven years that I prayed for her. I called her house to find that she was in the hospital. I asked my entire family to pray, and I went to visit her the next day.

I remember feeling the presence of the Lord as I walked the corridor of that hospital. I felt like I had angels ushering me into her room. I knew that I was on a mission for the Master! As I reached the door to her room, I stood there for a moment to make sure she recognized me. I had not seen her in over two years. She looked at me, smiled with tears streaming down her face, and said, "I'm ready to pray." I walked over to her bedside and explained the plan of salvation. As she prayed the sinner's prayer, her countenance changed and a glow came across her smiling face. The Lord had answered prayer! Edna was saved! She went against her son's advice after hearing about the gospel concert she attended. He said, "I don't want to hear about you finding religion." Thankfully, Edna didn't find religion, she found Jesus! She went to be with the Lord shortly after our move to Tennessee.

I can't help thinking that if God had answered my prayer the way I wanted Him to and when I wanted Him to, where Edna would be today. I was tired of waiting on God, but I now realize that in the "waiting-room" of my unanswered prayers, God has an eternal purpose and perspective on everything that involves His children. This particular time it was Edna.

When you are "waiting" on your answer and God has pushed the "pause" button, remember to be sensitive to the needs of others around you. They might be hurting too! They need you! They need your prayers and need to experience the hope that lies within you! Who else will show them? God may be calling you to be the one that points them toward the cross.

If we are constantly pointing others towards the Cross we will be too busy to focus on ourselves and our problems. God is asking you to reach out to others for HIS SAKE and for HIS GLORY! Isaiah 43:7 says that we were created for His glory. *"Even every one that is called by my name: for I have created him for my glory, I have formed him; yea, I have made him."*

Look for divine opportunities to encourage others while you are in the "waiting" room of life.

Cindy, Isaac, and Edna

Chapter 22

The Fear Factor

The word fear is a word that we hear more and more each day. We are inundated by the media, the news, and people with information, issues, and events that create fear.

A few years ago, there was even a television series called "Fear Factor." The contestants tried to overcome their worst fears by facing them.

Fear is defined as a distressing emotion aroused by impending danger, evil, pain, etc., whether the threat is real or imagined; the feeling or condition of being afraid. Synonyms: foreboding, apprehension, consternation, dismay, dread, terror, fright, panic, horror, trepidation, qualm. Antonyms: courage, security, calm, intrepidity (Dictionary.com).

We have all experienced this very real emotion at different times in our lives. Some of us might have a fear of spiders, of sharks, or fire, etc. Under certain circumstances, these are healthy fears.

Most of us have probably experienced the fear of an uncertain future. We worry about what tomorrow holds, or might not hold for us. If we are not careful, we will allow Satan to saturate our hearts and minds with fear, eventually living a life in bondage.

In 2005, I began experiencing an unhealthy fear. At times, I was afraid to leave my house. My heart would race rapidly, and for a while, I didn't realize that what I was experiencing was anxiety.

My life during this time was good. My days were filled with taking care of Isaac and my nephew, Gabriel. I was enjoying being a mom and an aunt and loving and nurturing my family.

One day, when I felt these feelings of anxiety come over me, I remembered 2 Timothy 1:7 that says, *"For God hath not given us the spirit of fear; but of power, and of love, and of a sound mind."*

That Scripture is proof that this type of fear is not from God, therefore, it can only be from one other source, and that is Satan. As we have discussed in previous chapters, we know from the Scriptures that the devil is out to destroy us and rob us of our peace and wants to take the joy out of living.

I remember very clearly when I was overcome by these feelings. It was at that point that I had recognized what Satan was trying to do. I had come so far since the death of Jacob, and I was doing great. I'm sure this made Satan angry, and he was bent on destroying my faith and my testimony.

I quickly determined that I was going to claim the victory over my situation. I put Isaac and Gabriel in their double stroller and began to walk up and down the streets of my neighborhood. I immediately began to pray and ask God for His divine help. He had helped me overcome thus far, so I was confident that He would do it again!

I prayed a prayer that went something like this:

Lord, you know I need you. I am crying out to you today and begging for your help. You have proven to be faithful to me in times past and I am depending on you to do it again. I need you to take these feelings of anxiety away from me. I pray this in the precious name of Jesus. I plead your precious blood right now, and I am claiming victory. I believe you are going to set me free from this bondage. In Jesus' name.

By the time I finished praying that prayer, I was already feeling better. I had felt the touch of the Master's hand. I began singing a song I remember learning as a child. I sang, "Once like a bird in prison I dwelt. No freedom from my sorrow I felt. But Jesus came and listened to me. Glory to God! He set me free! He broke the bonds of prison for me. Glory to God! He set me free!"

God instantly delivered me that day, and I have never had a similar episode of anxiety again!

The Psalmist wrote, *"I am the God that healeth thee."* Not only does He heal us physically, but He is able to heal us emotionally as well. He can heal our minds, freeing us from the bondage of fear. It's so easy to fall into this pit. But if we recognize what is happening and know that God is able and willing to help us, we can be set free.

God is able to transform every aspect of our lives. He is constantly reaching for us to rescue us, to heal and repair.

He is Jehovah Raphe which means to cure, or repair, to mend, to restore back to life (Psalm 41:4).

You may be dealing with a past filled with failures, afraid of what the future holds. You may be living a life blinded by your tears from years of disappointment. Your hope may be locked away by a heart that's full of fear. The chains of fear may be wrapped around your heart squeezing the breath out of you.

I have good news! Jesus wants to help you break out of the prison you are in. It's time to start living again! It's time to allow God to transform and renew your mind by His Holy Spirit. Isaiah 41:10 says, *"Fear not, for I am with you."*

Take a step in the right direction, and ask God to help you. Exercise your faith in Christ! Proverbs 3:26 says, *"The Lord is your confidence."* Recognize that Satan is your adversary, and he wants to make you feel trapped and defeated. He will lie to you, tell you that there is no way out, and fill your mind with confusion. Remember that God is not the author of confusion.

John 10:10 says, *"The thief cometh not, but for to steal, and to kill, and to destroy: I am come that they might have life, and that they might have it more abundantly."*

Take another step realizing that Jesus came and died and rose again so that you can live a life of victory. He holds the keys to death, hell, and the grave; and He holds the keys to unlock your prison doors of fear.

Once the reality of the cross is born in us, we can begin to SEE Him for who He really is. We have to believe that HE overcame death and the tomb so that we can receive the freedom from our bondage and start living our lives enjoying the abundant blessings that God intended for us.

John 14:27

*Peace I leave with you, my peace I give unto you:
not as the world giveth, give I unto you. Let not
your heart be troubled, neither let it be afraid.*

Don't allow fear to be a factor in your daily living.
Fear can keep you from your destiny. If you allow it, the
chains of fear can squeeze the life out of you. Decide
today to walk in freedom and live in the abundant presence of God each day with the blessed assurance that He
is with you every step of the way!

Chapter 23

The Forever Factor

"In my Father's house are many mansions: if it were not so, I would have told you. I go to prepare a place for you" John 14:2.

What we are experiencing now is not going to last forever. James 4:14 says, *"Whereas ye know not what shall be on the morrow. For what is your life? It is even a vapor that appeared for a little time, and then vanisheth away."*

Life is temporary and transient. The only thing that will last forever is where we will spend eternity. Eternity is certain. It is referred to as time without end. Death opens the door to eternity. Eternity in Heaven is inevitable for Christians.

There was a time, shortly after Jacob's death, when I actually questioned if Heaven was really real. I almost allowed my pain to extinguish my faith. I was struggling to believe, yet striving to reach for the promises in God's Word that pertained to the reality of Heaven.

When in doubt, we can look to God's Word! I'm so glad that I have God's Word to stand on because it tells me that Heaven IS real. We can choose to live like we believe it, or not. I choose to believe every word of the Bible from the front to back. We must live what we say we believe. If we portray that we believe the Word, but really don't, we will eventually betray what we portray.

Heaven is not just a pretty story or a fairy tale. It is a real place that Jesus has prepared for each of us that have accepted Him as his or her Savior. The Bible describes Heaven as a place where there is no sorrow, no pain and where there is no sickness! That's enough to make anybody want to go!

Heaven is a place that is filled with the light of Jesus. There is no darkness! It's a place that is filled with peace and happiness!

Revelation 21:4 says:

And God shall wipe away all tears from their eyes; and there shall be no more death, neither sorrow, nor crying, neither shall there be any more pain: for the former things are passed away.

One day we will all look back at our fiery tests and trials of life and say the same, "Each was just another bump in the road on our journey to Heaven." When we get there, the things of this world will not matter. Our trials will seem so small.

Where will you spend forever? If your answer is Heaven, then focus on the fact that now is not forever, and you can handle your disappointments with a different perspective. Let's use the time we have left to serve the Lord.

The Scriptures tell us that only what we do for Christ will last. Why not be the servants God intended us to be so that we can build up the kingdom for Christ? I encourage you to live your life on purpose, with a purpose! If you do, you will reap blessings of endless joy and peace in your life.

What is your purpose in life? What is your passion? What do you want to accomplish before you die? Is it to have material things and to enjoy doing what you like to do most? Or, do you intend to make a difference in this world by helping and encouraging others that need to hear the hope we have in Jesus Christ?

"Use me, Lord," has been my prayer since I began journaling in 1999, and my heart's desire since my childhood. This prayer was fulfilled in a way that I never dreamed. Every storm and every trial that He allowed was for my good. I am convinced this book would have never been birthed into existence had I not walked thru the valley of the shadow of death after Jacob left this earth, as well as experienced the mountain top when God fulfilled His promise by sending Isaac into our lives. The Lord has used both Jacob and Isaac's lives to bring forth a testimony of God's faithfulness and to bring glory and honor to Him!

God gives victory to those who will believe and to those who will give to Him their whole hearts and trust Him completely. We'll miss out on God's very best for us if we don't allow Him to be our everything.

Journal writing 7/7/13

Unless you give Me your whole heart, you can't receive all you need from me. Allow Me to consume every area of your heart and soul. Give me your wants, your desires, your dreams, and I will fulfill them the way that I see fit. Let me be your all in all and you won't be disappointed (spoken by the Holy Spirit).

As you yield your life to Him, you can rest assured that you will reach Heaven one day! Until the day we reach our final goal, we must keep pressing on. We can press on with His assurance and hold on to the promise of seeing our precious loved ones again. You will see your baby again. You will hold your child again, and the next time you do, it will be FOREVER! So focus on the FOREVER FACTOR!

I still miss Jacob very badly, and there are times I cry. There are different ways we can cry. In the beginning of my grieving process, I cried as if there was no hope. When I do cry for Jacob, I cry remembering that there IS hope. It's a healthy cry when we can remember that Heaven is just around the bend. Tears are a natural part of the healing process God intended for our lives. The following journal writing expresses my thoughts on this:

Journal writing 6/22/10 &3/31/12

Only Heaven Knows

Only Heaven knows what you would be,
If you were here with me.
Sometimes the tears will flow and I have to cry,
But not as if there is no hope, only for what I cannot see.

Only Heaven knows how many moons will have hung
In the starlit skies above before I see your precious face,
Or how many sunsets will kiss the earth,
the ocean blue,

The mountain peaks, until I hold you in
my arms again.

Only Heaven knows how many times you've been held
By Jesus himself, resting close to His bosom,
Listening intently to the rhythm of His heartbeat,
In sync with the songs of praises filling the air with
Adoration to the King of Kings.

Only Heaven knows how many times you've been rocked
By the angels above, being swayed to the lullabies
Sung by the Heavenly choir more beautiful that mortal
Ears have ever heard.

I am resting in the promise that I will hold you again,
Reunited and enjoying the sweet splendors
of Heaven together,
Hearts joined forever!
Singing with you our praises to the Master for
endless days to come;
Until then, I'll hold you in my heart,
While you rest safely in the arms of Jesus.

We all travel different roads on our life journeys. We all have a story. Will yours have a happy ending? You will be the one to determine that. I am certain that if you have made the choice to receive Christ as your personal Savior, your story WILL have a happy ending. When your life on earth is over, you will be able to enjoy the splendors of Heaven FOREVER; a brand new beginning that has no end!

You may feel like you have descended into the depths of the ocean, but you are never beyond His reach. Even in death, He is there to keep you. At the close of this life, you will be held up by His everlasting arms. Death will call us one day, but our Heavenly Father's eternal arms will prevent our fall no lower than the grave.

Charles Spurgeon

May we all determine in our hearts to make Heaven our final goal and set our eyes on an eternity filled with joy in the presence of Jesus! We have something to look forward to. The best is yet to come!

May your hearts be filled with an expected hope until He fills them with Heaven's best!

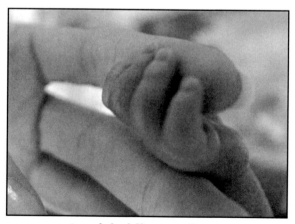

Jacob holding my finger

Chapter 24

Heart Songs

"And he hath put a new song in my mouth, even praise unto our God: many shall see it, and fear, and shall trust in the Lord" Psalm 40:3.

I have always had a love for gospel music. My family took me to every gospel concert in our area when I was a child. I sang with my parents in church and developed a love for family harmony.

When Jacob passed away, and nothing else would soothe my broken spirit, I listened to music. I spent hours upon hours listening to Christian lyrics and angelic harmony. The words of hope sank into the depths of my heart, and on many occasions, seemed to usher in the sweet Holy Spirit. It opened up my mind and enabled me to hear from God's Word. It helped me to focus on the positive and not the negative.

Music can calm a heart that is filled with turmoil. It has been proven to be therapeutic and is even used in helping people to learn to talk again. When listening to music, we use both sides of the brain. Patients with dementia can still remember lyrics and melodies of songs when they can't remember anything else.

Music goes deep into our innermost thoughts. Remember what the Scripture says, *"Out of the abundance of the heart, the mouth speaketh."* That encourages me to fill my mind with songs of hope, not songs that the world has to offer. There is so much emphasis placed on music in the Bible. As we mentioned before, David's songs on the harp were used to soothe King Saul. Music was used to bring the glory of the Lord with songs of worship.

Shortly after our move to Tennessee from Florida in 2007, the Lord began to do a new work in me. I woke up in the morning with my mind filled with melodies. I soon discovered that God was inspiring me to write lyrics for those songs. After we settled in our home in 2008, the Lord continued to pour these songs of hope into my heart. I penned my lyrics onto paper, but God engraved the melodies into my mind and onto my heart. What God started, He soon would finish. In the fall of 2010, someone suggested that I put my songs on a demo CD. After several months and the completion of the CD, I felt led by the Holy Spirit to record an album. After much prayer and thought, I began the long process.

My first CD project entitled "All the Glory" was produced in May of 2014. Since then, the Lord has opened several doors of opportunity for me to sing and share my testimony about His faithfulness. I am diligently working on another album entitled, "Reflections" from my

Journey to Joy. The lyrics to these songs are ones that I included throughout the pages of this book to further inspire and encourage the reader. I am thankful that the songs He has given me as a result of my "night season" are now being used to bring comfort and hope to others that are in need of encouragement. I must say that this part of the journey has been the most rewarding.

Journal writing 4/10/14

There is a song for every stanza in our life story. Many different melodies, according to what season we are in. But, no matter the season, God is gently arranging the most beautiful life song, eventually making all things new. Our "life songs" are filled with "rests"; times of waiting when God teaches us patience. They are filled with various "measures" of God's grace, yet always enough for whatever season we face during our "life song" journey.

Heart Strings
by Cindy Johnson 9/25/12

Words unspoken, yet you hear them
Tears are falling down like rain
Hearts are breaking, you can mend them
You alone know how deep the pain.

Refrain

Play your song upon our heart strings
Plan a melody of praise
Soothe our souls with hymns of worship
Take control, Lord, this we pray.

With tender care, ever so softly
You gently brush your loving hand
Across each chord, across our heartstrings
A melody never heard by man.

Isaac

Chapter 25

The "Call"

As I was praying before work one day, I heard the Holy Spirit speak very clearly to me for the first time. He said, "Don't forget the call I've placed upon your life. Yield yourself to me, and I will make a way." That happened many years ago in 1999, but those words still ring in my heart ever so loudly. I remember where I was standing, and I remember grabbing a yellow sticky note to write those words on. The note was destroyed in the fire; however, it will forever be engraved upon the tablet of my heart. I didn't hear an audible voice, but I knew it was the Lord speaking to me through His Holy Spirit.

When God speaks to you, whether it's through a Scripture in the Bible, or speaks something to your heart, you never will forget it, and you will never be the same.

The following journal confirms what I continue to feel in my heart and the season of contentment and joy that I am finally experiencing as I continue to yield to His will.

Journal 5/2/14

Today is Jacob's tenth birthday. For the first time since his passing, I do not feel a sense of sadness. I normally tend to feel a bit melancholy; however, I am experiencing a new season in this chapter of my life story. It's a season of joy and contentment. The Lord has turned my darkness into light and my mourning into laughter. With God's help I have endured the night seasons of weeping and pain. Joy has finally come! (Psalms 30:5) My circumstances have not changed; however, God has changed me and has given me an eternal perspective as I look towards the hills where my help comes from.

As I reflect on the days since Jacob's birth and home-going, I am grateful for the unsurpassable peace and uncontainable joy that Jesus continues to give me. I've had to brave the cold winter winds of pain to get to this part of my journey; however, this JOY that I have in my heart has made it worth every mile!

True joy lies underneath all emotions and is not based on circumstances. It's His Joy that sustains us and keeps us. It turns the depressed towards deliverance, and I have been delivered!

Psalm 16:11

Thou wilt shew me the path of life: in thy presence is fullness of joy; at thy right hand there are pleasures for evermore.

The Lord has called me out of my comfort zone to speak in churches as well as ladies' events. He has charted a new path for my family to minister together to share a message of hope to the hurting. Our desire is that others will know and experience the "realness" of

God in their storms. We want to proclaim a message that is reflected in the following Scripture:

Isaiah 61:1-3

> *The Spirit of the Lord God is upon me; because the Lord hath anointed me to preach good tidings unto the meek; he hath sent me to bind up the broken-hearted, to proclaim liberty to the captives, and the opening of the prison to them that are bound; To proclaim the acceptable year of the Lord, and the day of vengeance of our God; to comfort all that mourn; To appoint unto them that mourn in Zion, to give unto them beauty for ashes, the oil of joy for mourning, the garment of praise for the spirit of heaviness; that they might be called trees of righteousness, the planting of the Lord, that he might be glorified.*

I pray that you will experience God's grace and love, and that you will remember that you are not alone in this world. I pray this testimony of God's grace is proof that God is able and willing to set the captives free and give new life abundantly! I want hurting people to know that Jesus cares. I want the broken-hearted to know that Jesus heals. I want to shout it from the house tops that those held captive by depression, oppression, or anxieties can be set free and that true JOY is attainable through Jesus Christ!

Journal writing 10/1/14

Once we allow ourselves to become pliable in the hands of the Potter, He can begin His greatest work in us, creating a master design that He has had in mind since the beginning of time. He can take our broken pieces and make our earthen vessels beautiful reflections of His love and grace. He takes us from brokenness to healing.

There is no pain or tragedy that is in vain in the life of a Christian if we allow Him to write our life story. Sometimes when tragedy hits, it feels like the end; however, the Lord can turn tragedy into a door of opportunity for miraculous new beginnings!

Look for victory in Jesus! When you find it, you can lead the way for others to follow in your footprints towards their joy for their journey so that they can FINISH STRONG! Be strong. Be courageous! The Lord thy God is with you ... until the very end!

Lord, may we each surrender to the call that you have placed upon our lives to carry out the unique task you have for us to do for your glory, for your honor, and for your sake.

**"Faith turns fear into freedom and peace.
Grace turns heartache into ministry.
Love turns disappointments into hope."**
Pastor Randy Johnson @ valleyforgechurch.com

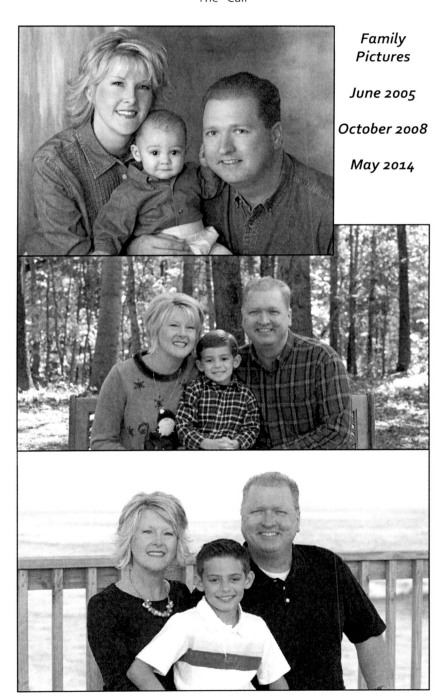

Family
Pictures

June 2005

October 2008

May 2014

Closing Thoughts ...

I am still learning how to walk in the ways of the Lord on a daily basis. I am beginning to see that *TOTAL SURRENDER = TOTAL CONTENTMENT and TRUE JOY!* This has proven to bring REVIVAL within my heart – a heart that was once dull and darkened by "self" gratification.

It has taken me years to surrender my "whole" heart to the Lord and I regret that I have been reluctant to bend to the Father's will. I am finally learning how to give Him my dreams and desires and how to lay aside my plans. I have slowly consecrated my heart to the cause of Christ, and I am now committed to the call and purpose He has for me.

I am learning to live FREE from "SELF" because I am learning how to submit to God's ways! There truly is freedom in submission! Being free from "me" and surrendering to His will brings great contentment. Yes, surrender = contentment! There's no other place I'd rather be than right in the center of HIS will where I can experience a joy that is not based upon circumstances.

Yielding to God's ways isn't easy and is a daily decision as we *deny ourselves*, take up our crosses, and follow

166

Him. I recall my mother saying many times that I was a strong willed child, and I believe that she was right! I am quite certain that the Lord Jesus knew and still knows that about me. Because of that fact, I can see now that the Lord had to break me ... break my will. Thankfully, the Lord Jesus has been faithful to me, patiently molding me and putting the broken pieces of my life back together. I am grateful that God takes our brokenness and makes us beautiful in the image and likeness of himself. When this happens, we are enabled to bring glory and honor to Jesus Christ as we choose to "pour" out what He has "poured" into our mended vessels.

As I strive to walk in the ways of the Lord and draw near to His heart, He fills me with such peace and joy that continues to overflow. He has proven to be real to me as I continue to bend my ear to His unmistakable voice. He is ever so faithful to me as I yield to His perfect will for my life. I have realized that I can do nothing in my own power, but only through Christ (I Cor. 4:13).

Journal writing 7/28/14

Could this really be a feeling of contentment inside of me? I've heard that Jesus is the only one that can satisfy this longing in my soul, and now I have finally found this to be true. He is more than I ever dreamed that He could be to me. He's more than I could have ever hoped for, longed for, or asked for. He truly is ALL to me! He has far surpassed my wildest dreams. My heart is constantly being revived with His joy and peace as I continue to dwell in the secret place of the Most High, basking in His presence and bending my ear to His voice of truth that sets me "free" from "me."

If only I would have surrendered to His will long ago. I'm sure I've missed out on many of the blessings that God had in store for me because of my strong will. Thankfully, I have learned from my mistakes, and I might add that I'm still learning.

Joy from a biblical perspective is not based on emotion. It's the kind of joy that is based on the attitude of the heart and not on circumstances. Joy is a wonderful gift that the Holy Spirit graciously gives to the believer in the midst of a storm when all seems hopeless. It's a joy that He alone can give which enables us to endure the darkest storms even when happiness has long faded away.

1 Timothy 6:6

But godliness with contentment is great gain.

Philippians 4:11

Not that I speak in respect of want: for I have learned, in whatsoever state I am, therewith to be content.

Isaiah 29:19

The meek also shall increase their joy in the Lord, and the poor among men shall rejoice in the Holy One of Israel

Nehemiah 8:10

The joy of the Lord is your strength.

Your Journey to Joy

John 10:10 Jesus said, *"I have come that you might have life and have it more abundantly."*

Joy is part of the abundant life that God wants for His children. When you become a Christian, Jesus takes up residence in your spirit. He brings with Him the promise of great joy! Sometimes, the trials and circumstances that we experience on our life journey weigh us down and even impair our vision of the promises of God. We begin to feel ourselves sinking into a pit of gloom and despair and before we know it we have reached bottom. We have the blues. We are depressed and maybe even oppressed by Satan himself.

I've got good news! The Holy Spirit empowers us and produces within us the characteristics of God and the gifts that He alone can offer. Not only does He offer us the gift of eternal life, but a life of freedom, victory, and unspeakable joy. This gift of joy is not based on circumstances. It is a supernatural gift that is real, plentiful, and powerful! It is up to us to receive this gift.

Imagine a beautifully wrapped present. It has a gorgeous bow on top, and it is wrapped in your favorite color. It's almost too perfect to open. Oh, but it's yours. This gift has your name on it! It's a personal gift to you from your Heavenly Father. You can claim this gift today. Make Jesus the center of your life and He will be the center of your joy. He is the giver of life and every perfect gift. It's time for you to unwrap the present and allow Him to fill your heart with His wonderful gift – the gift of joy.

The joy that Jesus has for you is the perfect prescription for the blues. You can't find it in a bottle or in your favorite department store. You can't drink your blues away. You can't shop them away or sleep them away. JESUS IS JOY!

Joy is reachable, it's attainable and possible in the life that is surrendered to the Savior! It's time to untie the bow and receive this gift of JOY! It's a gift that He keeps on giving until your cup is full and running over with abundant life!

How will your journey end? Will the end of your life journey on earth be the beginning of enjoying the splendors of Heaven for eternity? If you don't know Him today, you can if you will pray this prayer, or a simple sincere prayer from your heart. Cry out to the Father regardless of your situation, prayer does change things and people!

The basis of the Sinner's Prayer comes from Romans 10:9-10. *"That if thou shalt confess with thy mouth the Lord Jesus, and shalt believe in thine heart that God hath raised Him from the dead, thou shalt be saved. For with the heart man believeth unto righteousness; and with the mouth confession is made unto salvation."*

Salvation Prayer

Dear God in Heaven, I come to you in the name of Jesus. I acknowledge to you that I am a sinner, and I am sorry for my sins and the life that I have lived; I need your forgiveness.

I believe that your only begotten Son Jesus Christ shed His precious blood on the cross at Calvary and died for my sins, and I am now willing to turn from my sin.

You said in your Holy Word, Romans 10:9, that if we confess the Lord our God and believe in our hearts that God raised Jesus from the dead, we shall be saved.

Right now I confess Jesus as the Lord of my soul. With my heart, I believe that God raised Jesus from the dead. This very moment I accept Jesus Christ as my own personal Savior, and according to His Word, right now I am saved.

Thank you, Jesus, for your unlimited grace, which has saved me from my sins. I thank you, Jesus, that your grace never leads to license, but rather it always leads to repentance. Therefore, Lord Jesus, transform my life so that I may bring glory and honor to you alone and not to myself.

Thank you, Jesus, for dying for me and giving me eternal life. Amen.

If you just said this prayer, and you meant it with all your heart and have repented of your sins, the Bible says that your name has been written in the *Lamb's Book of Life.* You are on your journey to Heaven and your journey to true joy!

As you begin your new life in Christ, I encourage you to get involved in a Bible-based church that teaches God's Word where you can worship, praise, fellowship, and grow as a Christian.

I would love to hear from you as you begin your new life in Christ. Feel free to email me @
cindysunshinetn@yahoo.com
or visit
www.cindyjohnson4hisgloryministries.com.

"Mercy is God's way to help us out of our Failure.

Grace is God's way to help us out of Distress.

Faith is God's way to help us out of Doubt.

Hope is God's way to help us out of Despair.

Peace is God's way to help us out of Storms.

JESUS is God's way to help us out of Sin/Hell."

Assoc. Pastor Mark Potter @ valleyforgechurch.com